Do Tell - II

Copyright © 2006 Ray Ruby
All rights reserved.
ISBN: 1-4196-4319-3

To order additional copies, please contact us.
BookSurge, LLC
www.booksurge.com
1-866-308-6235
orders@booksurge.com

RAY
RUBY

DO TELL - II
From This Day Forward

2006

Do Tell - II

This Book Is Dedicated To My Beloved Wife, Jane, And All Of Our Children, Grand Children And Great-grand Children.

***

I Would Like To Acknowledge My Grand Daughter, Stephanie, For Her Valued Help In Editing My Manuscript—and For The Assistance From My Son Paul As He Helped Prepare My Work For Publication.

INTRODUCTION

This is a continuation of my book "Do Tell - Hear the Corn Grow," written due to the urging of family, relatives and friends so that they may learn the "rest of the story." It would take many, many pages to describe the antics of our eight children (much of which we probably do not know), their experiences, and accomplishments. In this book, therefore, I have touched only on the highlights. My hope is that sometime they may tell their own story.

FROM THIS DAY FORWARD

A bitter north wind blew flurries of snow into my face as I walked home from The North Side Bank on Friday, February 7, 1947. Normally, we didn't complete work on Friday until about 8 or 9 p.m.—but I was given permission to leave at 5 p.m. in order to prepare for the big day. Tomorrow, February 8, was the day that Jane and I would be married at the 9 a.m. Mass at Corpus Christi Catholic Church on Jennings Road. 'Home' was on Acacia Drive with Aunt Annie and Uncle Phil Deuser. This would be the last night I would spend there.

The weather report called for a continued cold front which would bring the temperature down to near zero in the morning. I was hoping for clear roads and no snow since Mom and Pop and my family planned to be there for our wedding, breakfast and the reception in the evening. I was particularly pleased that Pop was coming since he rarely attended such events. I wanted everything to go well for all. Uncle Phil offered his Buick Roadmaster as our wedding transportation and brother, Joe, would drive us where necessary on our wedding day.

I awakened early on February 8, pleased to find no snow, but the thermometer indicated 8 degrees above zero with a cold wind. I guessed we were all ready for the wedding Mass and that entire busy day. Brother Bob, best man, and cousin Harold (Mike) Maisak and friend Roy Duenke, my groomsmen, agreed to wear dark blue pin stripe suits, but they had been quite hard to find. The selection in clothing was still very limited although World War II had ended eighteen months earlier. It was necessary to do the best we could by borrowing what we couldn't find to buy or couldn't afford to buy. Bob borrowed a pair of black shoes from one of Mike's friends but they were a size or two larger than he wore. There was some concern that he could walk out of the shoes but, other than the odd appearance, all went almost as scheduled.

We arrived at Corpus Christi Church and were a bit shocked to find that the heating system failed during the night and it was nearly as cold inside as outside. Bob, Mike, Roy and I waited in the vestibule to escort the maid of honor, the bridesmaids, and of course, Jane, the bride. When Trudy Price, the maid of honor, came down the aisle, she cast a worried look to the vestibule since Bob had not moved. I nudged him to get started and he turned to me saying, "Ray, I'm not going to go through with this!" I poked him in the ribs saying, "Bob, you are not the one getting married, it's me, get going!" With that he moved out with a silly look on his face, but my attention was riveted to those large shoes, hoping they would stay on!

I didn't know if it was because of the cold but the Mass seemed rather long. I felt sorry for the girls since their exposed flesh was turning blue. I attempted to follow the wedding prayer given us, glancing frequently at the rest of the party. Bob seemed frozen in place and I notice he was still at the "Prayers at the foot of the Altar" in the prayer book while we were past the consecration. I discreetly pointed to the book, calling Bob's attention that he was running behind. He whispered, "Don't worry, I'll catch up!" He was at the offertory when the Mass was over! Father Blankenmeir gave us a final blessing so that we could go forth, be fruitful and multiply. We tried hard to live up to that blessing!

Father Blankenmeir felt badly about the cold church and compensated by having the church hall at 80+ degrees for our reception that evening. Our wedding was the first one in which photographs were allowed inside the church during Mass. They turned out well, but were a shadow of those made in more recent years. Our breakfast (dinner) was held at Heidelberg Inn on Bellefontaine Road. after which we drove to Rosati Kain to visit one of Jane's favorite nuns, Sister Henriette.

We left the reception at midnight, taking Jane's dad's car to their home at 8850 Jennings Station Road. There, we changed clothes and called for a taxi to take us to the Jefferson Hotel in St. Louis, where reservations had been made by a recent employee at North Side Bank. She told me that she was well known there and could get us a special rate. Much later, as I told her how gracious and accommodating they were at the Jefferson, she said, "Well, they should be, since I am a regular there, being escorted by dates paying from $50 to $100 for her services!" I was a bit shocked!

Well, the taxi driver got lost trying to find Jane's house but finally arrived. We then reached the Jefferson at 3 a.m. It was a long day! We attended the 8 a.m. Mass at the old St. John's Church then went by taxi to St. Louis Union Station, where we boarded a Pullman Coach for our honeymoon trip to Little Falls, Minnesota. DeWayne Schwanke and his recent bride, Milly, would meet us there upon our arrival at noon on Monday. Since DeWayne and I sailed together and I had met Milly in California, I would be with friends, but it would be a new friendship for Jane. An upper berth in a Pullman car was less expensive, so that is where we spent the first full night of our honeymoon. I would not recommend an upper berth honeymoon! Actually, I don't think I would recommend a lower berth either!

We arrived in Little Falls, all bundled up for Minnesota weather, and found DeWayne and Milly waiting for us, wearing just light sweaters! It was 20 degrees. The week was filled with exciting activities new to us, even ice fishing. We had a great time!

***

Jane's mom and dad fixed two rooms upstairs which we could use until we found a place to rent or buy. Rentals were almost non-existent and unless you had something the owner wanted, you could forget it. We bought a divan and chair and fixed up one room for a living room. The other room had a bed and dresser. Both rooms were unheated, but that didn't worry us. What concerned us, however, was the practice that Jane's mom had of placing newspapers between the springs and mattress to keep the mattress free of rust stains. We quickly learned that every movement in bed sent a rustling noise throughout the entire house! We moved the mattress to the floor!

We continued to look for a house to buy and wanted to find one for $7500 or less. I had sold my car, a 1942 Pontiac, for $1300 and would use this, a part down payment, should we find something. In late March, Aunt Annie told me that Herb Beimdiek had purchased three lots on Lexa Drive and had constructed three brick homes. The first was sold and the second home was nearing completion. They were all brick two bedroom, one bath and gas forced air heat. No garage or paved driveway. He wanted $9500, so I said we could not afford it! Aunt Annie said, "Nonsense, you can do it!" We looked at the house, liked it and wanted to buy. I checked with Mr. Naunheim, told him that we would have $2050 from the sale of my car, what I saved from the Merchant Marine, and wedding gifts. That would leave a loan of $7500. A 25 year FHA loan at 5½ percent would make the monthly payments $72.25 which would include taxes and insurance. My monthly salary was now $225, so I could qualify. Jane was working at the Records Administration Center, but her salary would not be considered by FHA or other lenders at that time.

It was then that I received a low blow. The sales of new homes were restricted to veterans only and they didn't consider Merchant Seaman who served in World War II as veterans! All branches of the armed services would qualify to purchase and receive a 4 percent GI loan though they may have never left their home state! I had spent my entire service, after training camp, at sea in either what was considered the war zone or battle area, on munitions ships or T-2 tankers carrying 100 octane aircraft fuel. One in thirty-two mariners on merchant ships in World War II died in the line of duty. This represented a greater percentage of war-related deaths than any other U.S. services. The government kept losses secret during the war so that they could continue to attract and keep mariners volunteering. It seemed we were ignored and forgotten! Mr. Naunheim contacted someone to complain and it was decided that I should be allowed to purchase the home. The next problem was simply my age. I was not quite 21 years-old and therefore could not legally make a loan! Thanks to Mr. Naunheim, both the veteran question and the loan matter was resolved as my friend and working partner, Ed Jezik, an Army WW2 veteran would take title and quickly convey the property back to us by Quit Claim Deed. Then in December when I reached 21 years of age, I obtained the 25 year, 5¼ percent FHA loan and we had a new house.

The great day arrived for our move to our new home. We had purchased a new stove, refrigerator, small table with four chairs and a mahogany bedroom set, all for about $655. We took the mattress and bed slats from the historic bed at Jane's mom's house. The slats didn't fit too well since the new bed frame was slightly wider. We thought it would work OK, but early in the first night in our new home, the bed collapsed. We again placed the mattress on the floor.

***

Jane continued to work at the U.S. Records Center and had accumulated $600 in her civil service retirement fund by the time she resigned. What a windfall! We bought a 1932 Chevrolet Sedan, in good condition, for $175 and put the rest in the bank! We now had transportation other than buses, streetcars and legs. When we learned that Jane was pregnant we felt we should try to find a newer car for safer conveyance of that precious new unknown. We found a 1940 Plymouth Convertible, sold the 1932 Chevrolet for what we paid for it, and bought the Plymouth.

Being unaccustomed to having babies, and reluctant to ask questions as to what to expect, I urged Jane to find out all she could from Dr. Weyerich, who would attend to her prenatal needs, deliver the baby and provide post delivery care for about six weeks for $100. She didn't feel comfortable asking the doctor questions, so we still didn't know anything. As the time drew close, I urged her to at least ask when we should go to the hospital. She complied and we learned that we should leave for the hospital when labor pains were ten minutes apart. The big night arrived and I was awakened by a loud ticking of a clock! Jane was sitting up in bed, holding our alarm clock. I said, "Are you having labor pains?" When she smiled and nodded yes, I asked how far apart and she told me eight minutes. We were not concerned since we thought we should wait until they got to ten minutes! When the next pains were seven minutes apart, we thought it didn't seem right so we called the doctor—WOW! He was upset so we rushed to the hospital.

Our first baby was born on February 24, 1949, and although the nursing hospital staff and the good nuns at St. John's hospital appeared to hate fathers, they allowed me to see our daughter! They held her up to the window and what a shock! This tiny creature was a miniature, 80 year old Granny Wilhelm, with a flat nose, wrinkled skin and plastered ears! I was sick! They signaled, through the window, if I wanted to see her again, I said "No!" Jane had not seen our baby yet and was anxious to learn what she looked like. I told her that she was really "something!" The next evening, at visiting hours, Jane was so excited since they brought our daughter to her and said she was a most beautiful child. I figured this was "mother's love" but reluctantly went back at baby show time to see our child. The nurse held up a beautiful little girl. We named her Rita. The lesson here is, "Never look at your new born children until they are at least a day old!"

As parents, our lives changed dramatically! We no longer remembered what a full nights sleep was like. We walked the floor for several nights hoping to comfort our crying baby, thinking she had what the book called, "colic." We thought perhaps she didn't like us or was just angry about something. Nothing seemed to work! We took her to the doctor and learned that Rita had an ear infection and must have been miserable! We were crushed that she was hurting and we didn't realize it! In years to come, we became experts!

I was so happy with our new baby and proud of Jane so I wrote the following poem:

The day dawned cold and dreary
On this February morn

But was lightened by our happiness
For our first child was born

This tiny babe you've given me
Is a treasure we'll adore
It shall change my life in just one way
I love you all the more!

The joy I've known since "baby" came
Is more than I can say
Much happiness is in my heart
And there shall always stay

My prayers are for you tonight
With my prayers to Him above
I thank you again with all my heart
For bringing us our new love.

God bless you, Jane, I love you
To our daughter you shall be
As wonderful a mother
As you are a wife to me!

Our first of many trips to Minnesota was made with Jane's folks when Rita was only four months old. We rented a cabin on Lake Alexander and enjoyed fishing with DeWayne and Milly Schwanke. As our families grew we continued our vacations to Minnesota. We rented a cabin at Island View Resort on Lake Alexander and when more space was needed, we rented two cabins. The rental was $35 per week and included a boat. We caught many fish and always had a great time. Jane's mother often commented that our trips to Minnesota were the best of her life. Jane's mother would watch the children while Jane and I fished early in the morning. I would then take the children fishing, take Jane's folks and finally Jane and I would fish until about 9 p.m. After two weeks we couldn't understand why we were so tired!

***

Since I was now making $275 a month, we decided to build a one-car detached garage. Bob, Boo, Joe and Ferd would build it so it would only be the cost of the material which they estimated to be $175. I made an FHA improvement loan for that amount with monthly payments to be $9.75 per month.

In January of 1950, I got a $35 a month raise! We now felt rich so we traded the 1940 Plymouth in for a new 1950 Ford sedan, costing $1635. They allowed us $800 for the Plymouth and we took out a loan for $835. We now had another payment along with our $9.75 improvement loan. Oh, the confidence of youth!

In April of 1950, we learned that Jane was pregnant with our second child. A beautiful round faced little girl, with the most trusting eyes, was born on December 27, 1950. We named her Jean! We felt truly blessed, for another beautiful healthy child.

OUR NEW BABY GIRL

On this clear cold night in late December -
With Heavens smile across the land,
You've given me a darling daughter –
A love that we can understand.

Thank you Jane, I LOVE YOU TRULY,
And this love grows through the years –
When "Baby Jean" says, "Mom, I love you"
It's payment for those painful tears.

I'd like to shout from atop a mountain –
I'm proud of Rita, Jean and you,
And I thank our God in heaven –
For making ours a love that's true

A love that's true shall last forever –
Built by our family, we hold so dear,
Each tiny voice that's added to it,
Shall make it stronger through the years.

Rita now was walking and climbing everything in the house. My brother, Bob, made a little stool for her so that she could reach the bathroom sink when we taught her to brush her teeth. On one Sunday afternoon, we were getting ready to visit some friends, and as Rita climbed on her stool to brush her teeth, she slipped and hit the sink with her teeth. When I picked her up, I was sickened, since her two front teeth were missing. We called Dr. Lambrechts and took her to his house on West Florissant. We thought the teeth were broken off, but when he examined Rita, he said they were driven up into her gums, out of sight! He told us that if the bud for permanent teeth were not greatly advanced, these baby teeth would work back down and no damage would be done. This is exactly what happened! The first of many miracles of God's love and protection for children!

A new interior paint came on the market which was "rubber based" and one coat would cover. It was sale priced, so we decided that we could afford to paint the plastered walls in the living room. We decided on a grey color and I started the project. Rita was under foot and reaching for paint, brushes and ladder. Jane saw how impatient and frustrated I was becoming so she decided to take the children to the drug store for an ice cream treat. I was pleased! Feeling that I should have shared in the treat, she returned with a grape Popsicle for me. I didn't want to stop painting, since I was on a ladder and cutting in at the ceiling, so I started eating the Popsicle with my left hand and painting with my right. Suddenly Jane yelled and I glanced down to see Rita climbing the ladder beneath me. I asked Jane to please do something with the child! I then dipped the paint brush, and shoved it in my mouth instead of the Popsicle. Rubber based paint tasted awful! I thought raising children was hard on nerves. Little did we know that it was just beginning.

***

With our new daughter, some extra expenses were now evident and the combination of the house payment, the car payment, utilities *and* the $9.75 garage payment left little. The

$9.75 garage payment was the payment that pushed us over the edge and if I could eliminate that, we would be OK. Having previously purchased one share of North Side Bank stock for $135, before we were married, and later having acquired a second share for $66.30 (due to stock split), I decided to sell same and pay off the garage loan. I approached Mr. Naunheim to find out what the stock was worth. He gave me a good hour of his time, explained the great value of the stock which would now be worth several times what I paid for it. I then told him I wanted to sell my two shares so that I could pay off my loan! He now gave me another hour of his time to convince me that at that time, the stock was virtually worthless! He said to hold on, since I would be considered for a raise in late January and could then handle the payment!

I then took a job on Sundays pumping gas for Barney Alderson at his Gulf Station on West Florissant and Lucas Hunt Road. He paid me $9 for eight hours of work which included oil changes, grease jobs and washings cars. When I accidentally drained the transmission oil, instead of the crankcase oil, in a customer's new car, I felt insecure with my lack of knowledge and thought I had best do something else. We convinced the customer that we changed the transmission fluid on new cars, without charge, in the event there would be metal filings left from the manufacturer. He seemed "sort of satisfied" but a bit concerned. I then did some bookkeeping for Barney instead of service work and still earned the $9 per week. In February, I got a $20 per month raise and we were OK.

Rita had difficulty adjusting to a new addition to our family, having moved from center of attention to sharing with Jean. At times Rita would be rough with Jeannie and downright cruel, taking her toys and pushing her away. I decided to talk to Rita and took her on my lap. I told her that children were a special gift from God and given to us to love and cherish. Each child was given their own Guardian Angel, who we cannot see, but are always with them. I told Rita that if she was not kind to Jean, the angels may take her away! This seemed to cause Rita some concern and she remained quiet for some time. Later, she asked me, "When do you think the angels will get here?" Rita adjusted to our new addition and continued to adjust as each new member arrived.

***

I continued to be active in all of the banking operations, except investments, having worked as bookkeeper, teller, note teller and loan processing as assistant cashier. Many episodes remain in memory of those early years but several in particular, always bring a smile and chuckle as I reminisce. Bank operations, in earlier years, were quite primitive and work intensive, not remotely resembling the banking operation of today. This was long before computers, microfilm, copy machines and printed checks, which meant all documentation was done by hand with a complex but accurate filing of records. Receipts for deposits and withdrawals were entered into the customer's bank book, and all deposit and withdrawal forms were retained in files. Saving account record of ownership was evidenced by savings pass books and verified by signature card. No withdrawals were allowed without first presenting the passbook.

The bank served an area populated by persons of diverse ethnical background with many, many, fine folks whom I came to know well and appreciate. One day, one of our Italian customers approached me with his savings pass book. He handed the book to me and said, "Mr. Rube, looka dat book—whosa name you see ina there?" I told him it was just his name. He said, "You dona see nobody elses name, eh?" I agreed and he said, "Now, Mr. Rube, looka that withdraw for $100 taka outa my book, I not do dat!" I asked him to wait while I retrieved the withdrawal slip from the files along with the signature card. I showed him the signature and withdrawal slip signed with what appeared as his signature. He said, "I not sign that slip and I wanna my money back!" I told him that he now had the savings pass book and that no withdrawal could be made without it and therefore he must know who signed the slip. He said, "I know who signa the slip—Momma, my wife, I keepa the book in my chesta drawers ina my room. Momma, she slippa ina my room, she sneeka my book, signa my name and taka my money! I wanna my money back!" I told him if his wife signed his name to the slip, that would be forgery and I would return his money but I would have to prepare an affidavit of forgery for him to sign. I would have the form ready the next day for his signature. When signed we would prosecute his wife for forgery. He asked what prosecute do to "Momma" I told him that she could be fined or even imprisoned. He said, "Mr. Rube, youa mean they may take Momma away!?" I said it was possible. He thought for a minute and then said, "You fixa the form, I be backa tomorrow, Goodabye Momma!" I had the affidavit ready the next morning when he arrived. He said "Mr. Rube, you gotta the form?" I told him yes. He said, "Teara the form up Mr. Rube, I talka to Momma last night, shea pretty gooda girl!"

Another incident also relates to forged checks which affected a traveling salesman. His checking account was only in his name and when we returned checks against his account for reason of insufficient funds, he contacted Mr. Naunheim, advising him that his wife could forge his name perfectly and wanted to keep his account but wanted to be protected. Mr. Naunheim decided to change the authorized signature by placing an 'x' after his signature. This worked for awhile and all checks without the 'x' were returned "signature not on file." Eventually the checks presented, started to appear with an 'x' after the signature. Many made to dress shops and other woman's apparel. We then went to two 'x's and a new signature card was signed. After a number of checks were returned, having only one 'x,' Mr. Naunheim received a call from the customer's wife. She snapped, "I'm on to you with your double x!" We suggested our customer try a different bank without telling his wife!

***

In August of 1951, we learned that Jane was pregnant with expected delivery in April or May 1952. We were thrilled and hoping for a boy to add to our beautiful family, while also hoping for an increase in salary to help with increasing costs. In January 1952, I was promoted to Cashier at the bank and received a raise. I was now making over $400 a month! With this extra income and feeling wealthy, my brother, Bob, and I bought a lot on Clearwater Lake for $300 and made plans to build a cabin for vacation and fishing.

Our first son was born on May 1, 1952, a beautiful boy with blond hair and a mischievous expression. We named him John. After John was born, Bob and I worked on the cabin on weekends, hoping to have it ready to use that summer or fall. It was a hot, hot summer. While working with Bob one hot Saturday, I developed a severe headache, became very weak and wanted some aspirins. We had none with us, and Piedmont was about six miles away. I started for town, but got only a mile or so and became violently ill. I stopped the car and lay on the side of the road for a long time before I could go on. I was suffering from heat exhaustion and didn't realize it. We learn from unfortunate experiences. We later furnished the cabin with surplus military bunk beds, a Coleman stove, lantern, and kerosene lamps. The cabin, lot, and furnishings came to $900. We would not get to use it until the spring of 1953, since Jane became ill with 'milk fever,' which ended our breast fed babies!

With Jane's illness, it was necessary to find help with the children during her recovery. Jane's Aunt Bertie Young agreed to keep Rita and my mom kept Jean while John stayed with Jane. After a week, Jane was again well enough so that I could bring the children home. Mom said that Jeannie was so well behaved; she hardly knew she was there. She would sit and play quietly while Mom and Pop worked in the garden. Aunt Bertie said Rita was so well behaved that she was no problem at all. It was good to have them all home again.

Our two bedroom home on Lexa Drive began to look a bit small, and we thought of trying to add on a room. All of our ideas resulted in a poor addition with significant expense. The house was not well designed for an addition. We decided to make it work with the girls in a double bed and John in a crib in the small bed room. Not much room left. We had to search for a larger home.

A residential development was under way in Bissell Hills with three bedrooms, one bath, and one car garage homes ranging in price from $11,250 to $13,000. We would have to sell our home before we could buy another, so we mentioned to neighbors that we wished to sell. A neighbor from across the street agreed to pay our asking price of $14,000 and we contracted for a home on Addison Drive in Bissell Hills for $11,650. The home had gas fired gravity heat, no air conditioning but an attic fan that worked great. We had a concrete drive but rock only in the garage. We moved to our new home on Thanksgiving Day in 1952. I borrowed Jane's dad's 1932 truck for the move with all my brothers helping.

In the spring of 1953, Bob agreed to keep John for us while Jane and I, with Rita and Jean, would check out the cabin and fishing in Clearwater Lake. Jane's mother made warm coats for Rita and Jean which made them look like refugees from the old country. The coats were warm, made with much love and we appreciated how she helped us with so many things. We spent the first few days of vacation at the cabin with the girls and I caught some beautiful crappie. We wanted Bob to experience the crappie fishing, so we drove home with our limit and talked him into coming down for the weekend. John's blond curls were now gone since Bob had taken John for his first haircut while staying with him.

Later that spring, my brother Boo (his real name was Leonard) helped me finish part of the basement in knotty pine and we installed a gas heating stove to complete a play room for the children. The larger home was timely, since baby number four was scheduled to arrive in August. As the time for delivery was drawing closer, we realized that we would need someone to care for the three children while Jane would be in the hospital. A stay at that time was seven to ten days. In mentioning this to Mr. Naunheim, he said his wife employed a girl named Jonnie to perform household chores and prepare meals. He would ask her if she knew of someone who would be interested. He learned that Jonnie shared an apartment with another black girl named Hallie and she would like to have the job. I called Hallie and told her the approximate date of Jane's delivery. On August 19, 1953, we had another beautiful baby boy! We now had it evened up with two and two. We named him Alan.

Before I called Hallie, I took Rita and Jean on my lap to explain that Mom had a new baby and that a nice girl was going to stay with them and cook their food until Mother came home. Since they had never seen a black person, I told them that Hallie was black but was just like us, so please don't say anything to her about her color, which may offend her. They seemed confused but promised to be very good. I drove into the black neighborhood to Hallie's apartment and knocked on the door. While waiting for an answer to my knock, a nice looking black gentleman came walking up the sidewalk to the apartment. He was well dressed with a flat 'skimmer' straw hat. He smiled at me and said, "Which one you waiting for?" I told him Hallie and was relieved to see him smile as he said, "Good, I'm here for Jonnie!"

Since there were few black persons seen in Bissell Hills at that time, I thought it best to tell my next door neighbor that I would be bringing a black girl home to care for the children. Her eyes widened and she seemed shocked, so I added that I would be sleeping in the basement while she was there. Her eyes grew even wider as she said, "uh huh!" Guess she didn't believe me.

Rita and Jean were very quiet when I brought Hallie home and introduced her to them. They kept staring at her but said nothing. Hallie was great with the children, so I was not too concerned about their silence. That evening, as we sat down to a nice dinner that Hallie prepared, I sensed that Jean was about to make some profound statement about Hallie's color. She finally spoke, "Howie, can I ask you a question?" Hallie said, "Why sure honey, you just ask me anything." Jean paused a minute, as I sort of held my breath, then she said, "Howie—

do you got a momma?" Hallie laughed and said, "Why sure I do honey, and you have a momma who will be back home with you in a few days!" All had smiles and accepted the temporary change without further concerns. All the while John sat in his high chair, eating well and being oblivious to any change in our household arrangements.

As the Christmas season approached in 1953, we prepared for our tree and purchased gifts for the children. We loved this busy time of year! It was then our practice began to put up the tree after the children were in bed on Christmas Eve, and arrange the gifts that Santa brought. At the bank's Christmas party, a few days before Christmas, I felt quite ill and left for home early. I thought I was catching the flu. The next day, which was Christmas Eve, I could not go to work but remained in bed. That evening as Jane started to trim the tree, I wanted to help, and tried, but could not manage being out of bed. After several days in bed, unable to eat, extremely weak and turning yellow, Jane called Dr. Sausville. He came to our house, took one look at me, and put me in the hospital. I had "Infectious Hepatitis." So New Years 1954 was spent in St. John's Hospital in St. Louis. The hepatitis left a negative effect which seemed to never go away. We learned that my sister, Mary, who apparently contracted the illness from the mental hospital where she worked, was in the hospital for a long time with this serious illness. My brother Tom also had the disease. We had probably given it to each other while visiting with Mom and Pop in Chesterfield.

With the four children, I wanted to buy a larger auto and looked at a new Ford station wagon at a dealership in Clayton, where a friend of 'Bo' Naunheim worked. The station wagon cost a little over $1900 and they would take our 1950 sedan in trade, and would call when the new car was ready. When they called, Bo offered to save me the trip by taking our 1950 Ford home with him and leaving his car with me. He would deliver our title and check to the dealer on his way home and the next morning, deliver our 1950 Ford to them, and pick up our new 1954. He called later that evening asking, "Ray is my car in your drive?" When I said it was, he said, "I'm so glad because someone has stolen yours!" He had picked up several bags of groceries on the way home, had taken one to his apartment and, when returning for the others—the car was gone! The dealer considered the trade completed, I assigned my insurance claim to them and they delivered the new wagon to Bo. Several weeks later, our 1950 was found having been used in a robbery. The Insurance Co. now owned the car. Bo complained bitterly about losing so many of his groceries! We still laugh when recalling the incident.

Time moved quickly while in Bissell Hills with Rita in kindergarten and Jane busy with all four. Rita got mud on her shoes and new dress for her first day in school and cried. A bad start for the school experience!

***

We looked forward to vacation in Minnesota with the children and always chose June for the trip. Jane would have everything packed, ready to leave when I got home from work on Friday night. We would fix a bed in the wagon so that all four could sleep, side by side, as we drove. Jane was always happy for the change of pace and scenery, even though so much extra work and planning went into the trips. We prepared for this year's trip and looked forward to going. When I arrived home, however, something was different! Jane was not smiling and seemed angry at me! I didn't know what was wrong or what I had done. She said she was fine! Finally, after my urging, she turned to me and said, "Who is Pat?" I was lost, didn't know, so I asked for a clue. She said, "Merchant Marine—The SS Whittier Hills!" The only Pat I could think of was a deck engineer whom I knew, so I told her, "He was a deck engineer!" She then shoved a letter at me and said, "Deck engineer, my foot, read this letter!" As she was packing for the trip, she found a letter in the side pocket of a suitcase which I bought in Calcutta, India.

I must relate this incident, to show how something, on the surface, can look so bad but can be totally innocent! It was Easter week when my ship, SS Whittier Hills, a T-2 Tanker, arrived in Sydney, Australia, after surviving several days adrift without power in a typhoon off the Great Barrier Reef. Since the Sydney papers followed the incident, we were some what celebrities when we managed to reach port on Good Friday. It seemed that everyone in Sydney knew about the Whittier Hills.

I wanted to attend Mass on Easter Sunday, so found the address of St. Mary's Cathedral, which adjoined a large park in Sydney. As I was walking through the park, there were several paths and I wasn't sure which would lead to St. Mary's. A girl approached on another path and I asked directions. She said she also was going to St. Mary's. She introduced herself as Pat Simms and we walked there and sat together during Mass. She knew I was from the Whittier Hills. After Mass, we left together. She and a girlfriend had planned a picnic for the afternoon, and suggested I could bring a shipmate and join them. Sounded like a good idea. Dick Haller, a seaman from our ship, and I joined the two girls for a picnic and visit to the Sydney Zoo. When we parted, I asked Pat if she would like to go to the Trocadero for the evening, a popular club in Sydney. She said, "Yes but I want you to know that I don't lay!" I was shocked and hurt when I told her that I would be a perfect gentleman and she need never worry about my intentions. We had a pleasant evening as she told me about her parents and how beautiful were the Blue Mountains, where her parents owned a cabin. We planned to visit again, but the next day I learned that the repairs to our ship had been completed and we would sail the following day to Brisbane to discharge our remaining tanks of gasoline. From there we would go to Bahrein, in the Persian Gulf, to load the tanker with crude and return to Sydney.

That afternoon I went to the department store, where Pat worked to say goodbye and let her know of our sailing plans. She said her folks had invited us to join them for a weekend at their cabin, so when I returned, perhaps that could be arranged. Since it would be winter in the southern hemisphere, she commented that I owned no warm coat. I assured her that my maritime peacoat would be fine. As we said goodbye and shook hands, (yes, shook hands!) I asked but one thing: "Have I been a perfect gentleman, as promised?" She laughed and said, "Yes,—darn!"

When we reached Brisbane, I received a letter from her, the letter which Jane now held in her hand and presented to me.

As I re-read the letter, I understood why Jane was so upset with me. It sounded very incriminating as I read: "I already miss you; have purchased a winter coat for you when you return. The arrangement for the cabin in the Blue Mountains is made. I'm sure you will like it and hope that you will like me a little. I'm looking forward to your return." Signed—Pat

We did hold hands as we walked from the Trocadero and I did shake hands goodbye. That is as intimate as we got and never intended anything other. Perhaps I could learn and remember how often I would rush to judgment.

Jane was quiet for a few days as we started on our vacation and I guess she accepted the truth I told.

Our orders were changed in the Timor Sea and we altered our course to the Fiji Islands. Never saw Australia again.

***

Early that fall, a policeman came to our house and asked if the little boy he had in tow belonged to us. It was John! They found him nearly a mile away, had taken him to the school, to see if anyone knew him. The little girl, who lived across the street, and attended the school, identified John. We didn't even know he was missing! This keeping track of children was getting difficult. Little did we know then, that it would become even more difficult with passing years!

One Sunday, our friends, Jack and Maxine Puhl, invited us to visit with them at Maxine's parent's home on Highway 30, south of St. Louis. They had a large yard, lovely home and we were enjoying a picnic there. While playing with the children in the yard, we noticed that Rita was missing. Just then a horn started blowing and we saw Rita running onto Highway 30. When I shouted, running to her, she ran toward an approaching car on Highway 30. I knew I couldn't reach her in time and suddenly she stopped, much too close to a tragic disaster. The picnic was over! We silently drove home, re-living the incident, where a small child can be playing nearly under foot and the next instant is gone! Thank God for guardian angels!

The Clearwater cabin was not working out as well as we had hoped. The distance was too great and the fishing had slowed considerably; also there was not a lot for the children to do there. Our last trip to the cabin was made in the fall of 1954. Bob had purchased a new fishing rod he wanted me to try. We packed the car on Thursday evening, so that on Friday we could leave right after work. Friday night bank work took longer than usual and it was about 8:30 p.m. before we could leave. We had fixed beds for the children in the back of the car and they were soon fast asleep. I was very tired after about two hours and asked Jane to drive. She was too tired and afraid she would fall asleep. We struggled on until we were about five miles from the cabin, on a gravel road, when the right rear tire blew out. It was a long and difficult task to change to the spare tire and when finished, I slammed the trunk and heard a snapping noise. I broke Bob's new rod! We reached the cabin about 2 a.m. and since it was quite cool, we wanted to build a fire in the stove before putting children to bed. Mistake! The warmth from the stove activated many red wasps which took more time to eliminate.

We finally made it to bed about 3:30am. I still wanted to fish, so I arose early and drove down to our boat which we had turned upside down and chained to a tree. Someone had shot a hole through the bottom! I returned to the cabin, got material to patch the hole, returned and launched the boat. Started to motor slowly across the lake while stripping out line, when a fast motor boat cut between me and shore and cut my line. I QUIT! Bob and I sold the cabin for $900!

***

A new parish was established for Bissell Hills just a few blocks from our house. We were pleased to be part of the new St. Jerome church. The church and men's club were bursting with new members. The pastor, however, was difficult and alienated many of the enthusiastic members, with us being a part of same. We longed to be back in our old parish of Corpus Christi, in Jennings. We also wanted a larger lot and space for the children to play and grow. We watched for Jennings property for sale.

We noticed the "For Sale" sign on the Ed Schreck property on Hord Avenue, and called the agent. This thirteen room house, built in the late 1800's and situated on over one acre was in almost original condition. There was also a barn, chicken house, carriage house, and garden and fruit trees. The asking price was $17,500 and we bought it after cashing out our Bissell Hills house for $14,000. It was the spring of 1955 and Jane was expecting our fifth child in September. Our new home had six fireplaces, one bath, an open staircase to the third floor, gas lights, stoker fired coal heat and high ceilings. It also had some small and possibly large ghosts. I will elaborate on the ghosts later.

The coal bin in the basement area had only a dirt floor, while the rest of the basement was concrete. The stoker fired furnace had been added at a much later date and apparently the house was originally heated by the six fireplaces and wood stove in the kitchen. I wanted to put a concrete floor in the coal bin before ordering the winter supply of coal. I called Fix Material to determine the amount of concrete needed and ordered same. I asked Bo Naunheim to help me with spreading concrete in the bin. We were ready, we thought! The concrete chute would enter the bin from the coal chute and we stood with shovels and rakes in hand. We didn't realize that the concrete trucks would pass under several large pear trees which were heavy with pears! The open receiver on the top of the truck scooped several bushels of pears into the concrete when they entered our drive. As the concrete started to pour into the bin, very fast, we frantically were shoveling and raking when Bo yelled "What the hell are those?" Looked like pears! They were! We couldn't stop since the concrete kept coming. The floor was finally finished and somewhere, in eight inches of concrete, was several bushels of large pears. Guess they are still there!

Ed Schreck told us that heating the house was relatively inexpensive, but he didn't tell me that they only heated *one* room and also burned logs in the furnace along with little stoker coal. Our experience was quite different, and the first winter coal bill equaled a month's salary. We planted a large garden, had great tomatoes, asparagus, lots of pears and bushels of apricots. The apricot tree was a fruit miracle producing more apricots than we had ever seen.

Our 'new' historic home had thirteen rooms, two of which were on the third floor together with an unfinished large room. There was no electricity on the third floor and very minimal electric on the second floor. Each of the six fireplaces had a separate flue but all were encased in a large chimney which extended about four feet above the roof. I knew that the fireplace had been capped off at the top of the chimney but wanted to see if one could be opened, the flu inspected and the fireplace used. We purchased a 35-foot ladder from Ed Schreck when we bought the property and it would reach to the wooden gutter on the south side of the house. I wanted it on the roof! Jane didn't think it was a good idea! I went anyway with Jane and Rita watching the ladder. My inspection of the chimney convinced me to leave the cap in place and get down off that roof. I was backing down when I started to slip—going faster and faster, as I heard Rita say, "There he goes, Mom!" My feet caught in the wooden gutter, saving me from a 35-foot fall. I never went on the roof again!

***

Rita had prepared for her First Communion and we invited Mom, Aunt Annie, Aunt Pauline and Aunt Tina for the Mass and dinner. We had assigned places in Corpus Christi and we had included Mom and Aunt Annie. Aunt Annie didn't show up, and we learned later that she thought it would be too crowded and started to the other low Mass, which was to be held in the church hall. On her way there, she fell and broke her ankle and was taken to the hospital. What started out as a beautiful day ended in sadness, but at the time we didn't know how bad it would become. On my way to the bank the next morning I stopped to see Aunt Annie and tell her how sorry we were to learn of her accident.

She lay in bed, looking very pale and complaining only about falling. She also said how warm and stuffy the room was. It didn't seem warm to me! I was at the bank a short time when Tom Kiefer called me to tell me that Aunt Annie had died. It was determined that the ankle break caused a blood clot and her death. I was deeply saddened in losing a person whom I learned to know and dearly love.

***

On September 14, 1955 our fifth child was born, a beautiful boy, whom we named Paul. When Dr. Sausville came to me, from the delivery room, and told me that we had another boy, he seemed as proud and pleased as I was. The boys now outnumbered the girls! Jane's mom offered to stay with the children until Jane was back home from the hospital.

When I came home from work, Jane's mom wanted to talk to me about Alan. She said he refused to go upstairs and take his nap. She said he was frightened of something in his room. His room, which he shared with John, was across the hall from our bedroom. The room at the end of the upstairs hall was to be the nursery for Paul and was the room nearest to ours. The girl's room was next to ours on the same side of the hall. I took Alan on my lap and told him we were going to go to his room so that he could take his nap. His eyes widened as he shook his head, saying, "No, no." I asked him why and he said, "There's a 'pook in my room!" I told him, no, there was no spook in his room and I would show him. He was not happy as I carried him upstairs. He clutched my neck as we entered his room and his eyes flashed all around the room. I told Alan to tell me where he saw the spook, so he pointed to his crib. I took him there and he pointed to the spot next to his crib where he said the spook stood. I asked him what the spook did and he said, "The 'pook just look at me!" I asked him what it looked like and he answered, "Like a 'pook!" He later told me it was a young boy, who stood by his bed and stared at him and then disappeared.

While we had heard many strange noises in the house, we attributed same to the age and size of the building. A number of times, I would be awakened during the night hearing footsteps which seemed to come from downstairs. When I went down, nothing was there, but then it seemed that footsteps were coming from the upstairs. The children would be asleep in their beds. Strange! Then one night, about midnight or later, Jane and I were awakened by a noise on the third floor, which sounded like someone plucking a guitar or banjo string. We both sat up in bed and Jane said, "That came from the (unoccupied) third floor, you have to go up and see what that was!" I said, "You mean WE are going to go up!" We took a flashlight and went to the third floor. The two finished bedrooms were completely empty so we opened the door to the large unfinished attic which was floored but nothing else. As I shown the flashlight around the room, I saw the chimney which served the kitchen area, and behind the chimney was a dark form. Closer inspection revealed an ancient, leather covered divan, of the type which could be opened for a bed. It had opened, and as we saw the rusty springs, we assumed that the catch had rusted through and released the bed, causing the twanging noise we heard. At least that is what we hoped. Much later, after the house was sold, we learned of many more 'happenings' which were experienced by the new owners. I will tell more about that later.

We continued improvements by changing the plumbing to the second floor bath, adding a shower in the basement, new wiring and electric to the third floor. I was concerned as to how we could get additional wiring to the second floor and wiring to the third floor, but Frank Barrett of Barrett Electric did a great job. The large cathedral-type doors, which separated the entrance hall from the front parlor, another which separated the front parlor from the back parlor, another which separated the dining room from the back parlor, and finally one which separated the dining room from the entrance hall, provided large pocket areas to pull electric wire. We now had additional electric to the second floor and electric to the third floor. Boo came out and installed a large window fan in the last bedroom at the end of the hall opposite the baby's room. Jane used this room as her sewing room. There was a small stairway at the rear of the house, from the hallway to the kitchen, which we rarely used. By opening the door to this stairway, the large fan pulled wonderful fresh air from downstairs to the upstairs bedrooms. Since there was no insulation in the walls, the large rooms with tall ceilings would have to keep the house comfortable on hot summer days and nights.

DO TELL - II

***

I continued my night courses which related to banking including Economics, Commercial Law, Negotiable Instruments, Real Estate Law, Consumer Credit and Effective Speaking. Eventually, I completed nine years of night classes. I wanted to be sure that I would have the necessary material to provide for our growing family.

In the spring of 1956, we learned that Jane was pregnant with our sixth child. We definitely needed a vacation that summer and planned to go to Minnesota in June. Since the garden would be producing, with asparagus and tomatoes and the apricot tree bearing, we asked our good friend, Bill Bandle, if he would watch the garden and use the produce so that it would not be wasted. He said he would be pleased to do so. He still talks about that summer! He said he didn't know that asparagus seemed to grow a foot over night, tomatoes by the baskets and never so darned many apricots. He was giving apricots to everyone he knew and was still deluged. When we now meet on occasion we have some good laughs about Bill's "farm experience!"

Early in November of 1956, on a cold night, we were awakened by a loud crackling noise in the house. As I leaped from bed, I could smell and feel the overheated air. As Jane rushed to get the children, I ran downstairs to hotter and hotter air! As I opened the basement door, the hot air was stifling, but still no flames! The furnace was cherry red with the stoker and blower going full blast. I shut off the stoker and blower but left the fan on to take out the heat. The controls had malfunctioned, and had filled the furnace with all the stoker coal, operating like a blacksmiths bellows! The crackling noise we heard was the wall paper separating from the walls due to the heat! After having all new controls installed for the furnace, I made rope ladders for the second floor and worried constantly about fire, fearing that it would be difficult to get all the children out in an emergency. The studs in the walls were 2x6 or 2x8 which ran from the first floor to the third floor. Without spacers or insulation, the walls would provide hundreds of flue chimneys. For peace of mind, I would either have to replace the coal fired stoker heat with a gas furnace, make some additional safety changes, or look for a different house. Another beautiful baby boy was born on November 10, 1956. We named him Gery.

When Gery was just a few weeks old, I took Rita and Jean with me on a Sunday afternoon to drive through Pasadena Hills, looking at houses. A 'For Sale by Owner' sign was on the home at 4505 Overbrook Drive, so we knocked on the door and met Mr. and Mrs. Spanos, who showed us the house. I liked it and told them that I would go and get Jane so that she could see it. I returned with Jane and the baby, leaving the others with Jane's mom. We liked the house and agreed to pay their asking price of $26,000 subject to our getting an FHA loan of $20,000. I was now Vice President of the bank and making $725 a month. With a year-end bonus my annual salary would be over $9000. FHA said I would qualify and our loan was approved. We bought the house and moved early in 1957.

Earlier in 1956 we sold our 1954 Ford wagon to my brother, Ferd, and bought a 1956 Rambler Station Wagon with three seats, the third facing the rear. It turned out to be a disappointing car. We also bought a used, orange Pontiac from Paul Frankowski for $500. With the two cars, we were now getting up in the world! Actually, I wanted Jane to have a car while I was at work in case of emergency, visiting her mom, or shopping.

The house on Overbrook, in Pasadena Hills was a very

nice house with three bedroom, 1 and 1/2 baths, two fireplaces, a completed room in the basement and an unheated large room over the two car, rear entry garage. I contracted to have a separate gas furnace to heat this room so that a fourth bedroom would be available for Rita and Jean. The neighbors ranged from very nice to strange. One was either giving gifts to Jean or telling the others that there was no Santa Claus.

On May 25, 1957, Boo and Trudy (Edeltraut Franke) were married at the St. Louis Cathedral and we had their reception at our house in Pasadena. All of our families from Chesterfield were there. Pop brought some of his prize strawberries for a special treat. We took a picture of everyone on the front lawn, and that is probably the only picture we have of Mom, Pop and the seven of us together.

While we liked the house, we wished for more space for the children to run. We looked for a place in the country for the weekends and vacation. A good friend and bank customer, Art Ochs, told me about a nice development south of Festus, Crystal City off Hwy 67, located on Platten Creek. His son had bought a lot there overlooking a ten acre lake. We looked at the development and bought a lot on the creek where the lake began. The children would be safe in the crystal clear water, which was only about two feet deep. We paid $900 for the lot.

Bob wanted to help me build a cabin and we began the foundation with concrete blocks. Bill Ahal, a friend, had removed some casement windows for an office building and gave them to me for the cabin. We completed a nice cabin of three large rooms and a full bath, in just over three weekends. It was designed for the main room of kitchen and living room to run from front to back, with windows overlooking the creek and lake. A long sleeping room for all the children was the same size on the west side, while our bedroom and bath was on the east side. We piped water from the creek for the bath and toilet and brought our drinking water from home. It was a great place and we all had enjoyable weekends and vacations there. Our good friends, the Bandles and the Wypers and their children joined us on occasion. The children re-named the "Country" to the "Fun Tree." Jane's mom and dad and Bob and his family, also visited and enjoyed this peaceful location. Jane's mom particularly liked the little stream in front of the cabin. Since the water was very clear, Rita would watch fish as they were on a nest and so often enticed them to bite. She became the most successful fisherman of us all.

***

In January of 1960, we learned that there would be another addition to our family. Jane was expecting our seventh child. I wanted to do something special for her for our wedding anniversary on February 8. I asked Jane what she would like for our anniversary. She said she didn't know but didn't need anything! Later that evening, Jane handed me the newspaper and pointed to an ad placed by TV station Channel 2. The ad read, "Win a two week cruise for two!" In 25 words or less, tell why you would like a cruise. I said sure, no problem, and continued reading the paper. She then brought me a pen and a used envelope suggesting that I write the 25 words. As a joke, I did, and wrote:

Wintertime dark-grey
Forces six inside play
Jangled nerves, what to do?
Quiet six—channel two!
Winters dragging—got the blues
'Sounds great—Tropic Cruise!'

I re-wrote it on regular paper and submitted it in Jane's name to the address given. About a week later, Jane called me at work to tell me that we were in the ten final considerations and they wanted to know if we could leave on a particular date in February if we were the winner. She said we could. They said we would be contacted, if we were the winners, before the announcement date on February 8. I told Jane not be too hopeful since the chance of our winning was remote! We heard no more from them! On February 8 the winner would be announced on the 6 p.m. Channel 2 Davy Crockett Program.

I suggested we not watch the TV, which was in the basement, since we would be disappointed, we sat down to supper. Finally Jane said, "Well, I'm going down to watch to see who won!" A few minutes later the children yelled at the same time the phone started ringing. Jane was the winner! The TV station called, friends called, we received a telegram advising us of the particulars. It was exciting!

I reminded Jane what I told her before we were married! "If she married me, we would go places and do things!" Well, we had been doing things so regularly that we almost eliminated the "going places" part. We now had a chance at that! We were invited to appear on the Jack Carney TV show on Channel 2 where we were given our tickets.

Jane's mom and dad agreed to stay at our house and care for the children and we left St. Louis on February 21 on the last flight out of Lambert Field due to snow and bad weather! The trip was everything they represented, with air fare to and from Miami, Florida, and two weeks on the SS Italia. We visited Port au Prince, Haiti; Curacao, Netherlands West Indies; La Guairá, Venezuela; Port of Spain, Trinidad; Bridgetown, Barbados; Fort de France, Martinique; St. Thomas, Virgin Islands; San Juan, Puerto Rico; and Port Everglades, Florida.

We met some interesting people on the cruise and more than a few phonies. No one knew that we had won the cruise and since we had nice quarters and I was a Vice President of a bank, they assumed that we had some money! Were they ever wrong! Some thought we were on a honeymoon! None knew that Jane was pregnant with our seventh child. Bo and Sue Naunheim arranged for a shipboard bar credit for us as a special gift. We had a grand time.

One of our acquaintances, from Southern Missouri, owned a barge company and in a conversation one evening, began talking about airplanes and flying. He noted, since I seemed interested in flying, he had a *real deal* for me. His company was trading in a Cessna 172 for a larger plane and he could offer the Cessna to me for $9000, a real steal. Was I interested? I told him that I would be, except for the fact that I had just put points and plugs in my used car and that this had set me back financially. He laughed, thinking this was a good joke. I laughed also!

The cruise was everything they promised and we had a wonderful time. We were invited to appear on the Jack Carney TV program on Channel 2 to describe our cruise. It was a nice experience for both of us.

***

Another beautiful daughter was born on October 1, 1960. Mary Kay was number seven and from early on she was most adventurous. Probably the cruise, of which she was not aware, instilled in her the travel urge. With seven children keeping us busy, our trips to our little cabin on Laguna Palma Lake were becoming rare. We decided to sell the cabin to my brother Bob at the cost we had in it. Bob and I provided all the labor in constructing the cabin and our cost was very modest. Bob and family enjoyed the cabin for quite a few years.

We still longed for a place in the country where we could eventually go, and started checking ads and talking to real estate agents about wooded acreage. We found 90 acres in Hawk Point which was all timber except fifteen acres in cultivation, but no buildings. It was owned by a banker in Hawk Point, whom I knew. He wanted $3500 with $1000 down and $500 principal each year plus interest at 5 percent for five years. We bought the property and paid it off in five years. The forest had been logged and was not as attractive when we could really see it the first winter. We later sold it for $7500. Today the same property would be worth at least $270,000. Oh well, my timing and the urge to always move on did not bode well for our making a profit!

***

Rita and Jean now attended St. Ann's Catholic School in Normandy, and John started kindergarten at Jefferson public school. When John entered first grade at St. Ann's, we were concerned since the teacher said he wasn't paying any attention in class. He surprised us all at the year end, since he remembered all that was taught. During his first year, Rita complained that John had a little girlfriend and was always holding hands with her, which embarrassed Rita. We told Rita and Jean that it was fine that John was nice to his little classmate. We finally saw her at Mass one Sunday. John's first girlfriend was a cute little black girl. He was full of surprises!

We still hoped to find some property in the country, where the children could have pets and room to roam, explore and play. We looked in St. Charles County and found 11½ acres on Gutermuth Road within a half mile of St. Joseph's church and school. St. Joseph's Parish. The pastor was Father William Pezold, Jane's second cousin. We bought the property for $8500 and started plans to build. Our good friend and my bank customer, John Adams, was willing to build for us and we were confident in John's honesty and building ability. We built a story and half brick home with a large screened in porch, with two car garage below the porch. Our walkout basement was finished for a recreation room which included a second fireplace. We moved to our new brick home in Cottleville in June 1961. Ed Hermeyer did the brick work on the house and the fire places. The fire place in the living room smoked and I asked Ed to check it out. He said he had built hundreds of fire places and this was the first one that smoked. We extended the chimney—it still smoked. I put glass doors on the fireplace and that helped. Ed then completed the fireplace downstairs and that one smoked also. I now had the only two fireplaces ever built by Ed that smoked! We didn't use them too much!

We had a natural spot for a small lake and had Lee Moorman build it. It was a beautiful lake about 1½ acres. We also had a small cattle pond on the upper field. We stocked both with bass and bluegill which gave us a great deal of enjoyment. The local conservation agent contacted us to become a model small farm. They would provide the plantings and we signed for 4½ acres as permanent pastures. They furnished multiflora rose, white pine, ladino clover and orchard grass. The pines didn't grow but the multiflora sure did. This plant became the scourge of all recipients of that aggressive bush. The birds drop the seeds and the thorny rose bush springs up everywhere.

Now, with Rita, Jean, John, Alan, Paul, Gery and Mary Kay, we still wanted to take vacations which we could afford and my love of fishing always directed such vacations to a body of water. We bought a three room tent with the necessary camping gear and made several trips to Missouri large impoundments. One such trip to Lake of the Ozarks started on a weekend in which we set up the tent and gear for Jane and the children while I returned to work, leaving Jane with the children. I would come back on Friday night and we could spend that weekend together. A big storm hit the area the night I arrived. Jane and I took the children to the concrete campground comfort station for safety. After the storm, we spent considerable time collecting gear and drying soaked sleeping bags and clothing. We decided this was not a good idea and we didn't do that again.

A cousin gave us a beautiful Beagle dog and we named him Duke Dog. He was a true loving beagle and a great rabbit dog. John Adams, our builder, had a 90 acre farm near Gerald, Missouri, and we had several great rabbit hunting trips there. When John decided he wanted to sell the farm, he offered it to us for $10,000. It was mostly open, had a small lake, a stream on the edge of the property and nice improvements, gas heat, knotty pine interior, one bedroom down stairs and a large sleeping loft upstairs. There was a large barn and an old caterpillar which John used for grading and building the lake. It also had the old original log cabin located near the house. The log cabin was in bad condition and would have to be torn down at some point. The house was furnished, including stove and refrigerator. We bought the farm. It turned out that we didn't get to use this property very much on weekends since the older children now had friends and playmates and their plans for weekends differed from ours. We later sold the farm for $14,000. Today, it would be worth at least $200,000. My timing and 'sell low' approach continued to keep us from becoming wealthy.

RAY RUBY

***

The children wanted a horse! I fenced the 4½ acres of permanent pasture and built a small lean-to type barn. Ferd had some used tin and material and helped me build it. We had one stall for the horse and manger with the other half for farm tools and the International Cub Tractor that Jane's dad gave us. Ferd said he could find a nice gentle horse for us, since he knew an honest horse trader (I now question 'honest horse trader').

We bought a pinto for $175 and named her Cheri-Babe. Wrong name! She was about the nastiest horse I've ever seen! She would bite, kick, ride you into fences and with the children in the saddle, would lie down and try to roll over them. When she tried this with Paul, I knew we must get rid of her. Then we learned that she was carrying a colt. Perhaps that was what made her so nasty! A beautiful colt was born and Cheri-Babe was now even nastier than before. Each time I suggested getting rid of her, Jean would strongly resist. One day, however, I was mowing the lower field with our tractor and asked Jean to open the gate to the pasture and barn. As she did, I drove through the gate and heard Jean screaming. Cheri-Babe was trying to run her down. As I jumped from the tractor, having thrown the tractor into neutral (I thought) it actually went into second gear. As my right hand touch the right tractor wheel, my foot left the clutch and I was thrown down on my back onto the belly mower. Feeling momentarily paralyzed I knew I must roll to the right or be crushed. I did just that, only to see the horse trying to step on me or kick me! I got to my feet, ran after the tractor, killed the ignition and held on to keep from falling. When I heard Jeannie yelling that the horse was after her. I ran to her to keep the horse away. My back was much more damaged than I realized and has plagued me ever since. That was the last straw for Cheri-Babe!

Although I wanted to shoot her, one of our neighbors wanted her and the colt and would trade a gentle older quarter horse for her. Her name was Ribbon. We made the trade and were pleased with this beautiful, gentle mare. Unfortunately, she developed an abscess on the frog of her left front leg which required vet service, followed by a daily cleansing of the deep hole in her hoof. This daily chore fell to Jane which she performed religiously until the abscess healed. Ribbon later ate too much green clover while it was wet with dew and foundered. This resulted in another of a number of vet bills which now totaled more than medical cost for all the children. Ribbon was never the same after being foundered, and when we looked out one very cold winter day and saw her standing in the middle of the pasture, covered with ice, stiff legged, unable to walk, we realized that we had to call to have her taken away. It was a very sad day!

***

We bought a 1965 Buick station wagon in the fall of 1964, just in time to bring our eighth child home from St. John's Hospital in St. Louis. We had another beautiful daughter born on November 25, whom we named Lori Rae. The roads were ice covered and very treacherous which kept our adrenalin high on the trip home with our precious cargo.

Our eighth child prompted me to write the following poem.

"TOGETHER FOREVER"

When the ring slipped on your finger -
And you softly said, "I do" -
And the Padre's solemn blessing -
Sealed our love so true.

Our life was just beginning -
Our ship upon the sea,
Now I thank our God in Heaven -
For the wife He's given me.

Each tiny heart that beats within -
Is filled with trust and love -
Each pair of lips we kiss good-night,
Is blessed by Him above.

Much happiness you've given me
Each day dawns fresh and new -
I realize it more and more,
I'm so in love with you.

And so, I'll say a prayer tonight
That we shall always be -
Together here upon this earth
And in eternity.

When the camping RV Show came to the Arena in St. Louis, we went to see what was offered, which could accommodate our family, and which we could afford. The Starcraft dealer showed us the Constellation model pop up camper and bragged that it could sleep eight! We told him if it would sleep ten we would be interested. He assured us that could be done by installing double hammock type bunks over each of the two dinettes. He agreed to do that and install brakes on the unit for the same price. We could manage the sale price and bought our camper! In the years that followed, we think we had more enjoyment from that Starcraft than the many other RV's we later owned. Guess it was due to the fact that all of our family was together.

***

In 1965 I was made Vice President of the bank and my salary improved. Uncle Phil Deuser invited Jane and I to dinner to celebrate my promotion at Norwood Hills Country Club. We joined Uncle Phil, his lady friend, his daughter Rita and her husband, Tom Kiefer. While seated at the table in their plush dining room, before ordering, I told a story causing all to break out in laughter. I was caught up in the laughter and leaned back in my chair too far. The chair tipped backwards and I reached for something to stop the fall. Unfortunately, it was the tablecloth! I pulled all water glasses, silverware, napkins and flower vase to the floor! The waiters were very gracious in cleaning up the mess. We all laughed about it, but I was embarrassed. Uncle Phil never invited us back, nor did any other members of Norwood Country Club!

Since Rita would reach her 16th birthday on February 24, 1965, and Jean her 14th on December 27, 1964, we wanted to do something special for them. With the new Buick we could comfortably make a trip to Fort Lauderdale, Florida, with just the two of them. A rare happening with our large clan! Jane's mom agreed to come to Cottleville and stay with the other children for the week we would be gone. The motel we selected was a bad choice with neglected maintenance, closed pool and shuffleboard. We made reservations at an exotic Polynesian Restaurant for the 24th, Rita's birthday. Upon arrival Jane and Rita got quite ill and couldn't eat. Probably a flu bug! The event didn't turn out as we planned, and I promised to make a trip to the beach when they felt better. The following day, both were feeling OK so we went to the bench and watched a dark, ominous cloud moving toward us from the ocean. I commented that if we were in Missouri, I would say that this looked like a tornado! As the wind increased, we left the area and returned to our hotel. It *was* a tornado which left wrecked boats and marina not for from where we planned to picnic. Since Rita and Jean both loved horses, we took them to Hialeah Race Track, only to be denied admission since they were both under 18. We told the gate keeper that we didn't want to gamble, but just wanted to see the horses—no deal! He was nice, but that was the law. We could still peek through the fence though, and probably see some horses as they came from the paddock. We decided the hell with the horses and Florida and came home!

With eight children, the cost of cars and education was always on my mind. Since I was now a Vice President of the bank and making $17,000 a year, but that salary would never suffice to provide college education for the children. At that time raises in the bank were quite modest and we could hope for no more than a $100 per month raise or $1200 per year. This concern nearly became an obsession.

Our nephew, George Musterman, had gone to work for a real estate developer, Al Mayer, and his first year in 1964 was an astounding success with the Mayer Company growing and expanding. They needed someone with management and financial skills. Al Mayer called me and invited me to lunch. He offered me a job as Vice President of his company, to be in charge of financial matters, land acquisition, zoning, etc. He offered to match my salary and pay a substantial bonus at year end, with the promise of significant salary increases each year. I felt I had to try, and accepted the position. Although it was quite a change from banking and a real challenge in land acquisition, I gave all my effort and launched into the job. I negotiated a more favorable rate on construction loans as my first effort, which resulted in a savings nearly equaling my annual salary. After two years my salary was $40,000 per year.

***

In June of 1965 we invited Mom and Pop for dinner and celebrate the children being out of school. Pop and I walked up to look at the lake, the pasture and the garden we had planted. I noted that he seemed so out of breath, but he said he was fine. Little did we know that on June 17 in the middle of the night, we would receive a call from Ferd that Pop had just died! As I drove to Chesterfield, I can't describe the ache in my heart! It would be the first of many, as each death diminishes a part of us. I arrived in time to see Pop being placed in the fire department's emergency vehicle and hear dear old Father Godfrey's comforting words. He had the greatest respect for Pop!

Mom would now be alone on their two acres but Boo and Trudy lived just across the road and would help all they could. It was the beginning of some lonely days for Mom and a sad time for all of us.

That fall my brother, Bob, son John, and I went deer hunting at Cordell Quetham's property in Texas County. We stayed in the old dilapidated farm house. Don and Leroy Mueller, Cordell, Bob, John and I had a great time but didn't get a deer. It was one of many future deer hunting trips with Bob and John. Gery, and Paul later joined us for some great seasons. All of which bring back the laughs, excitement and joy of being together.

***

In 1966 we planned a two week vacation to Florida in our Starcraft camper. We had a boat rack installed on the top of the camper and a storage box for our 18 horsepower Evenrude motor on the rear bumper. This meant, with the boat on the camper, it had to be removed before we raised the pop-up. It got to be a chore, but all assisted with setting up camp and departures. Each had their specific duties and did them well. The ten of us started on the trip. At only about 30 miles from home, I stopped the station wagon to move the 18 horsepower motor from the trailer's rear bumper to the inside forward part of the trailer since we had insufficient tongue weight which caused the trailer to weave. We selected Santa Rosa Island for our campsite, which has a beautiful white sand beach with water on each side. We launched the boat and set up camp. It was very nice until Mary Kay wandered away! We found her in a short time across some sand dunes. We then watched the younger children much more closely. We pulled the children on a zip sled behind the boat. John's turn came and as we were pulling him, a school of porpoise cruised near the sled. He thought they were shark and screamed to us to get him out of that water!

A three generation family selected a campsite next to us and started to erect their new tent. The grandma seated herself in a lawn chair to supervise and watch the tent set up. We took the children to the beach. When we returned another camper came to our site, laughing, and said he had to tell us about the erection of the tent. Throughout the setting up Grandma kept saying—"It just don't look right to me!" They argued that they were following instructions and it was the way to do it. She continued, "It just doesn't look right to me!" Finally, he could wait no longer and approached the team to tell them they had the tent upside down, with the floor forming the ceiling! She then said, "I told you that it didn't look right!"

We had budgeted $200 for this vacation, so we were very frugal in food purchases and campsites were generally National Forest, Parks or Corps of Engineer campgrounds. A special one time treat for the children would be stops at a fast food drive-in for hamburgers, fries and shakes. On that occasion, we ordered twenty hamburgers, ten fries and ten milk shakes. Alan accompanied me to the window and when I placed the order, the woman clerk asked me to repeat it, which I did. She then turned and yelled to a co-worker, "Mryt, get a load of this!" Alan was so tickled and said, "Dad, if we do this again, can I be the one to go with you?" Growing children sure have good appetites

On the way home, we stopped and camped on Corps property on Greers Ferry Lake. We had great fishing, and met some good friends. I would take two children at a time with me to fish. At Alan and Paul's turn, I selected a deep channel to troll for walleye or bass. Since I was running the motor and trolling away from the campsite, I saw only the opposite shore. We had two great fish already on the stringer, one being a 7+ pound bass caught by Paul. Suddenly, Alan said, "Dad the sky back there sure looks funny!" When I looked back I could see the trees being blown over on the far hillside and a funnel type cloud fast approaching the campsite. I had Alan and Paul lie down in the boat and hold on as I turned the boat toward shore. We were nearly there when the wind struck and turned our boat in the opposite direction. I kept steerage, made a large swing, kept the boat into the wind and waves and made it to our campsite by the shore. Jane was trying to keep the Starcraft from blowing over, since the awning was already blown down and gear blowing away. The storm passed quickly and all was well. We considered it to be a great vacation and arrived home within our $200 vacation budget. We decided that we would look for a more solid camper, although we really liked the Starcraft.

***

Bob, Ferd and I talked of buying some rural acreage together and we started our search. Ferd and I checked on a listed farm near Owensville. It had a small, well built house, a small shed and a large barn, situated on 200 acres of mostly wooded property. They wanted $15,000. We bought it and told Bob that he had a one-third interest in the farm. With Ferd and Bob's expertise we soon had the house and the barn looking great.

It was at this farm that we experienced an incident which ages parents and turns their hair white. We were at the farm with Ferd and our family and planned to leave for home about 9 in the morning. Mary Kay was gone! We called and called, searched around the house area without success. Ferd and I drove to Owensville and asked the Sheriff's office for help. A radio appeal went out and we were joined by many volunteers - some on horseback, the Boy Scouts, Fire Department and the Highway Patrol. We covered acres and acres of area, including abandoned farms, old wells—no Mary Kay! I rode with a state trooper and used his loud speaker to call Mary and asked her to yell if she could hear us. We drove country roads and lanes without a trace. Our hearts were heavy and I had the sick feeling of fear and anxiety that I would experience other times in the future! It was nearly dark, when a farmer pulled his pickup truck into the yard and he had Mary Kay! He found her walking on a gravel road about 3 or 4 miles from the property. She had gone into the woods by a small wet weather creek near the house, wandered too far, became disoriented and walked the wrong way into the many hundreds of acres surrounding our property. She was trying to grin and cry at the same time. Again we thank God for guardian angels!

After the house was broken into and being stripped, even to bed linens and dishes, we decided to sell. We then sold 80 acres to two of my friends from the bank, divided into two 40 acre parcels, for $8000. We then finally sold the 120 acres with the improvements for $35,000 and divided the profit.

***

After three years, I was becoming disillusioned with the Mayer Corporation, since Al Mayer and I had a difference of opinion on financing arrangements and pricing structures of homes to be sold. I resigned!

We planned a vacation to Minnesota, while I decided what course to pursue for employment. I was considering my own real estate brokerage since a highly qualified real estate secretary would be interested in joining me should I make a change. Before leaving for Minnesota, I had a phone call from Bill Courtney, president of a bank in Mexico, Missouri. He wanted to talk to me. We scheduled a visit and I met with Bill Courtney and two of his bank directors, Colonel Stribling of the Missouri Military Academy, and the President of the A.D.

Green Brick Company. Mr. Courtney was ready to retire and wanted to take a long vacation to Europe. We discussed the bank for several hours, after which he offered me the president's position on the condition that I would buy his one-third stock interest in the bank. I told him that I didn't have that kind of money and could not afford to buy his stock. Bill said he understood that may be the case, so he would personally carry a 100 percent loan on the purchase, with the interest rate to be equal to the amount of dividends paid on the stock, and the principal would be an annual payment equal to my annual bonus as president of the bank. I could hardly believe this most generous offer. I told them that we were leaving for Minnesota in a few days and I would call him when we returned. He then gave me the banks profit and loss statements for the past five years so that I could determine the bonus that I would be paid on the bank's profits. I thanked all three for the opportunity to visit with them and drove home with many thoughts running through my head!

While in Minnesota, visiting with a war time buddy and family, I had a call from Bo Naunheim, President of North Side Bank. Bo wanted to know when we would be home since he wanted to meet with me and talk. Upon our return, Bo had arranged a dinner meeting with all of the bank directors. They wanted me to come back and offered a satisfactory salary, plus title of Executive Vice President. I was pleased to be coming home to an environment with which I was quite familiar. I returned all bank records to Bill Courtney along with a letter of appreciation of his offer and my decision to return to my familiar surroundings. He was most gracious, saying he understood and respected my decision.

***

Rita graduated from St. Dominic High School in 1967

and was awarded a full four year scholarship to Fonte Bonne College in St. Louis. She interviewed and decided that she didn't like it. Said the people were snobs! She turned the scholarship down and we registered her at St. Mary's College in Leavenworth, Kansas. After completing one year, she did not want to go back and returned home, going to work at City Bank and Lindberg Bank.

Jean graduated from St. Dominic's in 1968, enrolled in Nursing College in Alton, Illinois and worked as a counselor at a summer camp Minnewanca in Michigan. Alan entered St. Henry's minor seminary in Illinois and would graduate from there four years later having made many life long friendships.

We bought a 17-foot Lil Hobo travel trailer and prepared for a trip to Montana to visit the Northwest and Glacier National Park. Since Rita was working at a bank, Jean at camp in Michigan, and John wanting to spend the summer working on a farm with his friend in Cottleville, we would only have Alan, Paul, Gery, Mary Kay and Lori with us. We could still manage in the 17-foot trailer, and our good friends Tony and LaVerne Schnelle would be traveling with their trailer, joining us along the route. We now had a Pontiac Station wagon equipped with car top boat racks so we could take our aluminum boat with us. All interesting sites were visited along the way and we finally arrived at Glacier National Park. We camped at Apgar campground so we could fish on McDonald Lake. Alan caught a very large lake trout, Paul fell in the lake while watching us land the fish, and we had a grand time. Tony was upset since we allowed the three boys to sleep in a pop up tent while camping at Glacier. He was correct; we didn't realize the danger of bears in the park. Fortunately, all worked out OK. They now would not allow any camping unless you were all in a hard sided vehicle (no tents).

It was a long drive on a gravel road to Lake Bowman, in

the northern part of Glacier, but we went there anyway to see that part of the park and to fish the lake. We were the only ones on the lake and Jane and I took Mary Kay and Lori on the first try at trolling for Dolly Varden's. The area was beautiful and we (or rather Jane) caught our limit of beautiful Dolly Varden's. I had little time to fish, since I was either netting a fish for Jane or preparing for the next one. When we reached the shore near our campsite we were approached by a game warden to check our catch. We proudly showed our stringer with our limit. He said, "They are all illegal fish!" I couldn't believe it and showed him our licenses and fishing regulations. He then pointed out that in the back of the regulations there were special rules for Lake Bowman and all Dolly Varden had to be over a certain length; ours not meeting that requirement. I apologized and asked what he wanted us to do. He said since we were camping right there, to fry the fish and have them for our supper. What a great guy, I could breathe again, since a fine for that limit of fish would have been impossible for us to pay!

After burning out a wheel bearing, and nearly losing a wheel, we traded the Lil Hobo for a 21-foot Fan travel trailer. We took a vacation trip to the great Smokey Mountains and camped at Bear Paw campground off the Blue Ridge Parkway. Everyone was anxious to get out, move around the campground and play, but I decided to move the trailer in order to see the sunrise over the mountains.

As I drove around the campground loop, the hitch broke and the trailer broke away, but the breakaway switch locked the brakes on the trailer. Hook up wires were dangling and our air lift shocks were ruptured! With the help of other campers, we detached the trailer and drove our station wagon to a blacksmith in the village. He was a great guy, very skillful, and working to near midnight, repairing the hitch. While watching him, he noticed that Alan and Paul had a bad case of poison ivy on their arms and necks, which they encountered a few days before while hiking in the mountains. He asked if they would like to get rid of the ivy. It was a resounding "yes!" He took them to a barrel, filled with water and covered with scum. It was the water in which he plunged heated metal to temper and cool. He told them to stick their arms into the water and then splash some of the water on their necks and where ever the poison ivy was evident. They looked at me and said "Dad?" I told them to go ahead and they did so. The next morning the itching was gone and only a trace of the poison ivy was showing. In a few days it too was gone!

***

When Rita bought a different car, we purchased her little Chevrolet for John, since he was now over 16 years of age. I came home from work on a rainy Friday night and asked why John was not at home. Jane said he had gone to a visitation at a funeral parlor in St. Charles to pay his respects for a good friend who had accidentally drowned. I had a strange feeling, mixed with considerable concern and told Jane that I wished he was home! Shortly thereafter I received a frantic phone call from one of the members of St. Joseph church telling me to come quickly since John had been in an accident. I told Jane to stay with the children and I drove to the site. John's car was in a ditch, had rolled against a telephone pole, had the roof caved in and John was still inside. Several people stood on the bank, fearing to go to the car. I rushed down the bank to find the roof smashed against John's head! His head was turned sideways against the back of the driver's seat. A small amount of blood was in the corner of his mouth. I got in the passenger side and pressed my back against the roof to take away the pressure on John's head. He was unconscious! A few men then came down the bank and, since the windshield was out, stood on the hood and helped me raise the roof enough to free John. At this time I heard Father Pezold's voice. He had waded in about a foot of water to reach the car. He said, "Ray is this John?" When I said it was, he placed his hands on John's head, said a prayer and then said, "John will be alright!" I believed him while realizing that, I had failed to say a prayer.

Father Pezold was a priest who will always be loved and respected. We consider him our personal saint. I rode with John in an ambulance to St. Joseph's hospital in St. Charles where Jane and Rita joined us. John was in a coma and the doctor had told us that the longer he stayed in the coma, the more difficult a recovery would be. We could detect no physical injuries other than a small bruise, about the size of a dime on his right temple. John regained conscious on Sunday and we brought him home. Thank God for miracles for large families!

We had the wrecked car towed to our property. It was a total loss and John was greatly depressed. I though it would help if I could find another car for him. My former secretary offered a little MG to us for $300 and we bought it. A few weeks later John swerved to miss a dog on Highway K and wrecked the little MG. Our nerves could not handle any more excitement so we decided that John would have to buy his next car himself.

***

When a friend approached me to be a builder, saying that

Rich O'Brien had eleven lots in Florissant that he would sell to me for $71,500, finance the whole balance and release each lot for $6,500 when the construction loan was opened

It sounded like something I wanted to do, and did it! We built ten homes on Tamzine Court in Marietta Subdivision at prices from $29,500 to about $37,000. They all sold, but the eleventh lot was a problem. We approached another friend, Don Young, a builder, for assistance. He then became a part of my operation, which we had incorporated as RAJA, Inc. with $30,000 capital stock which represented all of my savings. I should have stopped there, but Leonard O'Brien offered 60 lots in Hidden Lake and Don Young was anxious to expand. I bought and financed the 60 lots and built three display homes. The day we opened the displays, the newspaper headlines announced the beginning of the most severe recession in years. It was as though the lights were turned off. We struggled to sell about 20 houses by taking in trades and doing what ever was necessary to create activity. The payroll, overhead and carry costs were great. We realized that we should sell our home in Cottleville and buy one of our houses in Hidden Lake. We listed our home and 11 acres for $49,000.00. No Takers! We then sold off five acres with the little barn, for $10,000. Finally we sold the house and balance for $39,500 and bought one of our homes at 1818 Lakeheights for $30,115 and moved on December 8, 1969. I would then be close to our bad investment and could assist, hopefully, with moving the 'spec' homes.

It was a difficult move for the children, especially for Gery and Mary Kay. Mary Kay had to leave her imaginary friend, Cheyenne, who apparently lived in Schulte's woods in Cottleville. Gery had to leave his friends in Cottleville and was bitter about the move. Years later, he told us that it was good for him that we moved. It was in Hidden Lake that he met a cute girl who, years later, became his wife.

Paul joined Alan at St. Henry's seminary in 1969; Jean again filled her summer vacation at Camp Minnewanca, and later, by invitation, returned as nurse in the summer of 1973. John graduated from St. Dominic's in O'Fallon, in the spring of 1970, joined the army and was sent to Germany for two years. Rita was employed by City Bank and Lindberg bank. Our house occupants were getting fewer.

***

We often visited our good friends Dr. Don Callahan and his wife Sally. Don was an enthusiastic private pilot and owned a six place Cessna. We flew with them a number of times; including a winter flight to New Orleans. I made many trips with Don and he encouraged me to take flying lessons and become a licensed pilot. At that time, a small fixed base operator had one plane at Lambert field and operated as Gateway Flying Service. He offered ground school and 40 hours flight time for $650. It seemed such a bargain that I signed up. His one plane was a Cessna 150. When I had 4 hours dual training we landed at Smart Field and taxied to the ramp. He got out and told me to take it around the patch. With adrenalin high I made my first solo! Gateway purchased another Cessna 150 in which I spent many hours, not realizing that his plane was in less than top shape. Little things such as engine failure over the Illinois River and quirky radio function!

On my first solo cross country, I was directed to Decatur, Illinois, which should be done strictly without radio navigation. I misread some landmarks and thought that I should be near the Decatur Airport, guessing my good time credited to a good tail wind. I couldn't find the airport! I finally called the Decatur field and told them that I was a student pilot on my first cross country and I should be over their field, but couldn't see it. I gave them my coordinates and they told me I was 20 miles southwest of their field and gave me the proper heading. When I reached the area where the field should be, I still couldn't see it and radioed to them. "We'll turn on the field lights for you." They did and I landed without mishap, refueled, had my log book signed and was cleared for take-off. When in the air, I radioed the tower to thank them for their help. They acknowledged and "told me to get home safely." I was embarrassed and upon reaching the Alton field, I asked for clearance to land. I was at 3000 feet! They gave me clearance then asked if I intended to land from up there. I answered no and requested a go-around to come in at the proper altitude. What a nerve racking trip!

On a later solo flight, I was returning to Lambert when my radio frequency to Radar went out. I tried the tower frequency and it also was out. In desperation I tried ground control and made contact. I told them the problem and they agreed to bring me in on their frequency. Such happenings would not be allowed now and student pilots are not allowed to use Lambert. I completed my flight hours, had previously passed the ground exam, and finally took my check flight with an examiner and received my private pilot's license! I was proud and wanted to take Jane on a short flight. We decided on Rolla and return. We had a snack at Rolla and after take off, as I banked to the left to get on course, my door flew open and all maps, papers and navigational charts flew out. I think they could have heard Jane scream at the Rolla field! I got the door closed and returned home without incident but Jane did not have much enthusiasm for flying!

I had checked out in a Cessna 172 and now could accommodate three passengers. Bo was anxious to fly with me, so I chartered the 172 and invited Rita and Jean to go along for a flight to Greers Ferry Lake. I had the fixed base operator top off the fuel the night before since we wanted to leave early the next morning. I did the pre-flight and Bo checked the fuel tanks. He asked where the fuel should show, since it didn't appear to be topped off. I thought it was OK (big mistake) and we left Lambert Field. At Batesville, Arkansas, Bo reminded me that the fuel gauge was showing close to empty. Since I estimated a surplus of fuel for an addition hour, after reaching Heber Springs, I was not concerned and also knew the fuel gauge was not too reliable in this older Cessna! We planned to circle the lake several times to see the sights, but I developed a crushing headache and felt I should land and take some aspirins. I radioed for clearance for a straight in and landed at Heber Springs. We rented a car and drove to our trailer. After taking some aspirins and sleeping for awhile, my headache disappeared.

Since I instructed the base operator to top off my tank, he anxiously told me that I had less than one gallon left when I landed! I couldn't believe it when I confronted the base operator at Lambert; I learned that the operator had leased the plane for one hour after he had topped it off. The guardian angels were with us. Thank God!

A friend of mine, Bill Stevens, who was a professional pilot, asked me to accompany him to Salt Lake City, to pick up a Cherokee Six, which his company had purchased, and help him fly it back to their base at Smart Field. Since Alan was home at that time I invited him to join us. We flew commercial to Salt Lake City and stayed overnight at a motel. The next morning we completed the transaction for the purchase of the Cherokee Six, checked it out, topped off the fuel and departed.

We agreed that Bill would fly the first leg to Scotts Bluff, Nebraska, and I would fly the last leg to Lambert Field in St. Louis. We had to go that route due to the altitude limitations of the Cherokee. We refueled at Scotts Bluff and I took the controls for the last leg. About an hour into flight both Bill and Alan fell asleep.

As I passed over an airport in Kansas, I woke Bill and suggested that we land and refuel knowing that we would need to do this before reaching St. Louis. Bill said no since he could buy fuel from a small fixed base operator just inside the Missouri border. I continued to fly and they went back to sleep. Shortly thereafter it was necessary to select a lower altitude due to increasing clouds since we were flying VFR rules. The weather seemed to continue to deteriorate and I woke Bill again and commented on the weather.

We picked up the weather station which was reporting isolated thunder storms which appeared to be out of our flight path. Bill said we would be OK and just continue the course. I was now down below 3000 feet. Suddenly without warning, it seemed as though a giant hand grabbed us and we were in the center of an imbedded thunderstorm! I could hardly believe the altimeter which shot from 300 feet to 8000 feet as lightning flashed all around us and wind and rain battered the aircraft! I told Bill to call Kansas City radar for a vector into Kansas City. He said "We don't have enough gas to reach Kansas City!" We had two main tanks and two wing tanks, all of which I had drawn down as I switched the weight of fuel! I had difficulty keeping the wings level due to the great turbulence and berated myself for having Alan along in the back seat. I asked Bill to fly the aircraft and I would work the radios. He did. Bill said we'd be OK since he could land at this fixed base field blindfolded since knew it so well! He finally made radio contact with his friend at the field to tell her hat we were coming in.

She shouted into the radio, "Bill, don't even try it, there is a tornado right on the field!" The radio was filled with the messages of other aircraft requesting vectors to some safe area. We had no choice but to hope there would be an opening and somewhere to set the plane down! I watched the fuel gauges and wanted to switch tanks again but Bill said we'd have to run the tank dry before switching, which would mean a stall in this turbulence. Not a comforting thought! Visibility was zero. If we could see the ground and find any farmers field or flat area we would set the aircraft down! Suddenly, a hole opened in the black mass and I could see the ground! I shouted to Bill that I could see an airport off to our left. It was the Columbia Regional airport. We requested and received a straight in landing. As we taxied to the refueling station we saw men standing on trucks watching the tornado we just left. Alan and I were the first to reach the bathroom since we thought we needed that!

When refueling was completed we found that we had no more that ten minutes of flight fuel remaining! I didn't want to fly the last leg to St. Louis but Bill insisted that I do so. He said it was like falling off a horse and you would have to get right back on. I didn't see the similarity since the ground was much closer from a horse's back, but I did fly the rest of the way to Lambert field.

This episode and some other experiences caused me to lose my desire for flying and I made few flights after that. Again, I thank God and His guardian angels for looking out for His children!

***

Alan graduated from St. Henry's Prep and entered Southeast Missouri State University in Cape Girardeau, Missouri. Paul left St. Henry's after two years and completed high school at Rosary High School in Spanish Lake. While there, Paul starred in the school production of 'Fiddler on the Roof.' He did an outstanding job, as did all the participants. Those who saw the production still tell us about it years later. The team recreated the production later in 2000 and was even better than the first time. We were quite proud of our gifted son and all of our children.

Gery, Mary Kay and Lori attended school at Our Lady of Loretto Elementary School in Spanish Lake as Paul graduated from Rosary in 1973. Alan and Paul wanted to hike the Appalachian Trail, since they had witnessed a little of its beauty during an RV trip made previously with the family. Don Callahan agreed to fly them to the starting point at Elligay, Georgia. We invited a friend, Kathleen Struckoff, to accompany us, along with Rita, Alan and Paul. Don asked me to fly and the six of us, with Alan and Paul's gear, landed safely at Elligay field where we waved goodbye to the boys. The trail was an experience that only they can tell, so they will have to write their own story.

"It all started here." Ray and Jane—February 8, 1947

We need more room!—Rita, Alan, John, and Jean

DO TELL - II

Our 13 room house in Jennings - shared with some small ghosts!

Alan, John, Paul and Jean—Pasadena Hills

DO TELL - II

Jean, Rita, John, Alan, Jane and Paul—Minnesota

John, Jean, Paul, Alan and Rita—Laguna Palma

Watermelon time—Jean, John, Paul, Alan, Gery and Rita—
Laguna Palma

RAY RUBY

Back Row—Alan, Jean, Rita and John—Front Row—Paul, Jane and Gery

DO TELL - II

Our home in Cottleville

Alan, Paul, Gery, John, Rita (holding Lori), Mary Kay and Jean

DO TELL - II

Jane and Ray with Lori

RAY RUBY

Mary Kay and Lori

DO TELL - II

Lori and Mary Kay with our lamb

RAY RUBY

Lori, Jean, Alan, John, Mary Kay, Rita, Paul and Gery—
Lakeheights

DO TELL - II

Family photo from 1973

RAY RUBY

Gery, Paul and John on "The Deer Hunt"

Alan on "The Moose Hunt" in Montana

John with deer and coyote—Owensville

DO TELL - II

Gery with bass from our farm lake

Mary Kay riding "Quick Draw" at rodeo

DO TELL - II

Mary Kay, Gery and Lori

Our home at the farm in Farmington

Lake and farm view in Farmington

Smoke house at the farm

DO TELL - II

Jane's fruit cellar at the farm

RAY RUBY

Farm girl—Jane

DO TELL - II

Rita and Jean

Rita, Ray and Jane

DO TELL - II

Jane and Lori

RAY RUBY

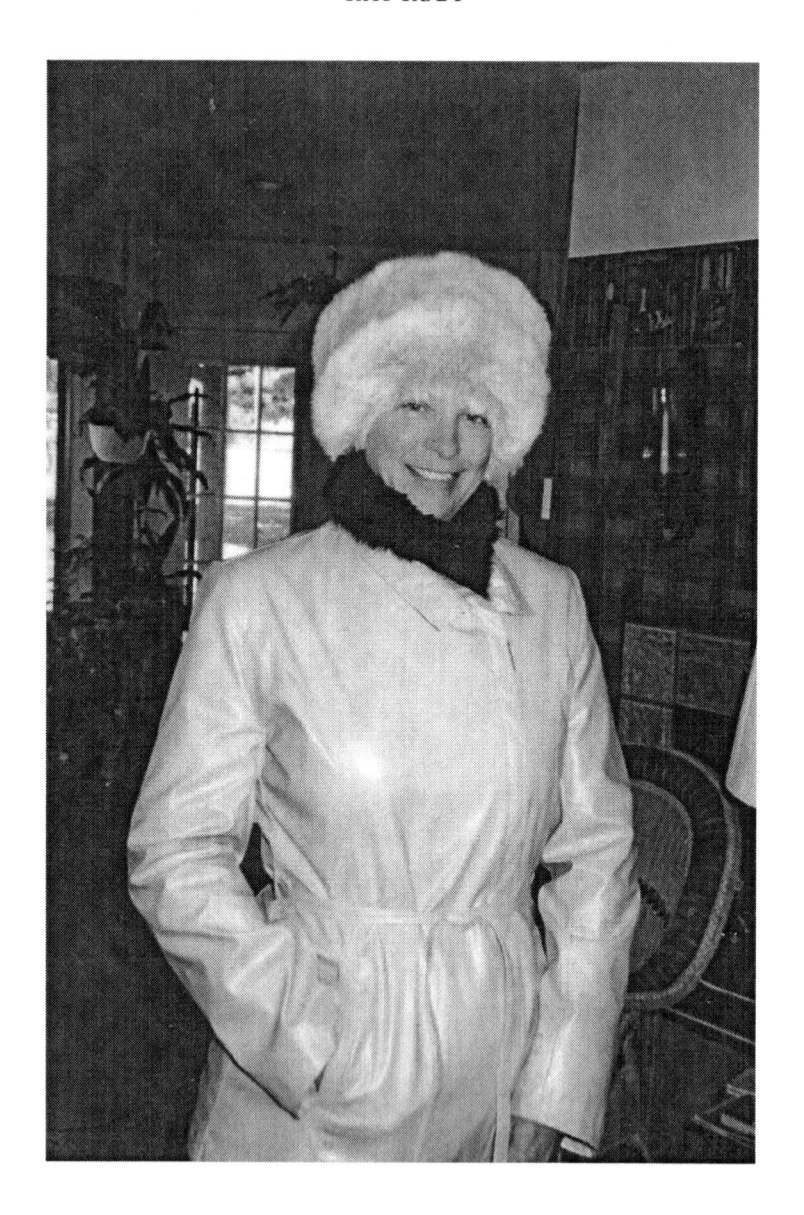

Mary Kay

Jean with Yoda and Patch

John at his farm in Minnesota

DO TELL - II

Alan

Our winter home in Yuma, Arizona - in the foothills

Paul on Memorial Day—2006

Gery on Memorial Day - 2006

DO TELL - II

Lori on Memorial Day—2006

Family at our 50th Wedding Anniversary

Ray and Jane 50 years from February 8, 1947

Our present home in Jonesburg

We took our 21-foot Fan trailer to a rented site on Greers Ferry Lake and arranged to leave the trailer there. We also rented a larger boat to accommodate more people and decided on a Pontoon Boat. In checking the boat dock for possibilities we learned that a 40-foot houseboat was for sale. We looked at the house boat and had the owner demonstrate for us. We bought the boat! We didn't examine the top deck closely enough and later found, to our disappointment, that the owner had covered some dry rot on the overhead with furnace tape and painted over the taping so it would not be easily seen. It had to be repaired so we arranged to fly our friend and builder John Adams to inspect the boat. The entire top deck had to be removed and replaced with marine plywood and then covered with fiber glass. John and his wife Eleanor agreed to use our trailer while doing the necessary work and he did great job.

***

Our good friends, Tony and LaVerne Schnelle visited us at Greers Ferry and enjoyed the fishing and houseboat. Shortly thereafter Tony was diagnosed with cancer and, after a long illness, passed away. Next to my brothers Tony was the best friend I ever had and also a great fisherman.

***

We decided to treat three special nuns to a weekend on the houseboat. The good sisters had never experienced a weekend such as that. We cruised about 20 miles up the lake and tied the bow to one of the exposed submerged trees and dropped our anchor from the stern. We swam, grilled hamburgers, and had a great time. A nasty storm came up during the night and I spent the most of the night checking our ties and anchor.

Thinking that the good sisters would have been frightened and awake most of the night, we were surprised to see them bright eyed and fully rested in the morning. They slept like logs and never even knew it had stormed. It was a fun weekend.

***

The Vietnam War was in full operation and we fully expected John to be sent there. We were surprised when he was sent to Germany and would be stationed in Geisen, not far from Frankfort.

Various suppliers, for our Hidden Lake construction project, awarded us a trip to Denmark. We wrote to John and gave him the dates we would be in Copenhagen, and asked if there was some way we could meet while we were in Europe. John managed a furlough and met us in Copenhagen in September 1971. He had purchased a Volkswagen and drove there from Germany. Jane and I, along with two friends from Illinois, crowded into the Volkswagen with John and toured a good part of Denmark. We had a fun time and it was good being with John.

Jean received her Nursing Diploma from St. Joseph's Nursing School in Alton, Illinois, in 1973 and began her nursing career. We were proud of her accomplishments.

***

In 1973 we looked for some acreage in the country and found a wooded 90 acres parcel on Knob Lick Road near Farmington. We bought the property for $15,000 and began building a road and clearing for a home site. This was to be the place where we would spend the rest of lives. It didn't work out the way we planned! We started some clearing where we would build our home and had some work done on the road to the building site. My back injuries were giving me great problems and we delayed building a barn with some basic living quarters.

In June my back problems became nearly unbearable and Don Callahan recommended Dr. Lattinville, a neurosurgeon. After viewing my x-ray, he said back surgery was the only option. I had ruptured discs which, in addition to the pain, were causing a paralysis in my right leg. We scheduled the surgery and Jane wrote to Alan and Paul on the Appalachian Trail. They discontinued their 1000 mile hike and returned home. I think they had covered nearly one-half of the trails.

The surgery was performed in July and was followed by a long healing process. The pain was gone! Dr. Lattinville recommended water therapy and, when we told him of our RV on Greers Ferry Lake he urged us to go there and do as much gentle swimming as possible. Dr. Callahan flew Alan and I down to Heber Springs and I tried to follow Dr. Lattinvilles's advice. While there, Joe and Joan came for a visit. I decided to take them for a tour in our house boat. When we were about ten miles up the lake, I suffered a severe headache so we started back to the dock. The headache worsened and I experienced nausea and weakness. I knew that the others would be unable to do the tricky maneuvering of a 40-foot houseboat, with a crosswind, to enter the boat slip, so I managed to dock the boat. Joe and Alan tied up and I felt my system going into shock! I was rushed to the hospital emergency, where we spent the night. The next morning I improved and was released. Since Jane had not accompanied us on the trip, she was unaware of any of my problems

Some friends from Alton, Illinois, Jim and Rita Voss, came to visit and we were surprised to see them. After that episode, I lost interest in the houseboat. Bo Naunheim suggested that

I donate the boat to an auction for the benefit of his children's school. I had several appraisals made of the boat and donated it to charity. My life pattern of "Buy High, Sell Low" continued! Since we no longer had the houseboat and the children had other interests, we stopped going to Greers Ferry Lake. I borrowed George Musterman's dump truck and pulled our 21-foot Fan trailer home. We then sold the Fan to a friend of George for $2000.

***

Rita and Jean were not satisfied with their work and decided to move to California. They chose Sacramento since I had once mentioned that I liked that city. Jean purchased a used Buick from Harry Adams and rented a U-Haul trailer. They had both car and trailer stuffed with their possessions as they pulled out from our home in Hidden Lake. It was a sad day for me!

John didn't want to live in town so he was staying with friends in Cottleville. Alan was in college and working during school break. Paul had signed up for a six year enlistment in the Navy which would begin February 14, 1974. When Alan returned to college in the fall our family of eight would be reduced to three. Gery, Mary Kay and Lori! After so many years seeing ten people around our dining table, the reduction made us keenly aware of our shrinking family. In December of 1973 I wrote the following poem and sent it to Rita and Jean with their Christmas gifts:

MY LITTLE ONES

Tonight the world seems cold and still
All blanketed in snow
My thoughts go back to the yesterdays
That seem so long ago.

I see you playing in the yard
Building forts and castles too-
Bundled in those funny coats
That Grandma made for you.

Or cuddled in my fishing boat
Eating cakes and jelly beans
Or climbing over fences
In your tattered Western Jeans.

The picture of our family
I see them—one by one
I've held them—hurt or sad
And see them having fun.

Jean defending 'Cherri Babe'
Johnny talking like a duck.
Rita catching all the fish,
And I astounded at her luck.

Gery searching in the woods

And busy—Al and Paul
Packing their foot lockers –
For St. Henry's in the fall.

Mary's secret friend, Cheyenne
Who lived in Schulte's woods
Never could I see him
But often wished I could.

In Lori, I see Jeannie
She's never gone away.
And was that Rita on her bike
Or really, Mary Kay?

My heart was nearly breaking
The day we said good-bye
A tear or two was choked away
But Dads should never cry!

I know it's true that all must change
As Summer into Fall
But you will always be my 'little ones'
You haven't changed at all!

***

John married Sue Hlavaty on Feb. 2, 1974 and found a place to rent in St. Charles County. Rita met and fell in love with Steve Ullrich from California and planned a fall wedding. Steve's father came for their wedding at Our Lady of Loretto church on September 21, 1974. We had the reception at our home on Lakeheights. Steve's father stayed a few days after the wedding, and we took him to see our property in Farmington. We had contracted for the half mile road into the site where we planned to build. No buildings were constructed at that time.

Alan wanted to complete the Appalachian Trail hike, so in the summer of 1974 he and a friend hiked the upper half of the trail which began in Maine.

I found a well driller who still used the old churn drill and had him drill a well where we would build our home. We found an unlimited supply of water at 143 feet. Since we did not have electricity, at that time, we rigged the old fashioned well bucket to draw our water. Now that we were satisfied that we had good water, we started construction on a pole barn. Bob and I built the barn with a completed loft that would serve as a rustic area to live on weekends and vacations until we built our house. We furnished the loft with beds, table, a propane gas stove and a wood burning heating stove. It was comfortable and we enjoyed many weekends there. Our little out house was built about 50 feet behind the barn.

***

In January of 1975 I was elected President and Chief Executive Officer of Charter Bank of Jennings. The Charter Corporation based in Kansas City had bought The North Side Bank, Bank of Overland and Bank of Ladue and all the bank names were changed. We found the Charter team easy to work with and formed many lasting friendships.

One of our bank customers who did volunteer work for the Red Cross told me of their efforts to find sponsors for Vietnamese families who had fled Vietnam. Jane and I discussed their need and decided to help. We had completed the lower level of our home into several rooms so we would only need to furnish beds and chairs. A family would have their own privacy and could take their meals with us. The walk out basement opened on to a small covered patio to the back yard. It would be a comfortable place for a small family until we could find a permanent home for them.

We agreed to sponsor and learned that our responsibilities would be to find permanent housing, employment, schooling, driver's license, acquaint them with our customs and assist them in any way to their new country. We were notified that a family of four would be assigned to us and that they would arrive at Lambert field on a Sunday around noon. Our Red Cross volunteer agreed to meet me at the airport and assist with the introductions, etc. Jane wanted to stay at home to complete the meal for our new quests. We had baked a ham and Jane had prepared all the trimmings.

We met the Pham family at the airport, Ninh Hu Pham, his wife Tinh Ti Pham, their daughter Cam Li Pham and nephew, Mi Hu Pham. I'm sure they were apprehensive and somewhat frightened, but we saw them relax as we exchanged greetings. We were quite pleased to find the Phams to be a delightful family and our friendship continues to this day. We did all that was required for sponsorship and the family adjusted well to their new surroundings. Lai would only be five years old on Christmas day so she would not start kindergarten for another year. Mi was ready for college and we decided to enroll him in the Florissant Valley Junior College. He could ride one the children's bicycles when weather was decent and we could manage to get him there in inclement weather. We asked Alan to take him to the college to register, since, at that time, the family possessed somewhat limited English. Alan relates the episode with some humor!

The name "Mi" was not a common name in our language and often created some unusual questions. Alan approached the registrar with Mi Hu Pham and told them he was there to register Mi, nodding in Mi's direction. The registrar asked Alan for his name. "Oh it isn't for me, it's for Mi. It began to sound like an Abbot and Costello "Who's on first" skit. All the while Mi stood grinning. They finally got it all worked out and Mi began his college career and excelled in all courses. At a Vietnamese picnic in Forest Park we met an Ozark Airline pilot whose church had sponsored a Vietnamese family. He told us that a college in Kansas City was offering a full four years scholarship to any Vietnamese student. We took Mi there for an interview and successfully obtained a full four year scholarship which included room and board. This was something we were unable to obtain for our own children but was pleased that Mi would get a good education.

Tinh was so gracious and wanted to do all the household chores, making Jane nervous. Jane wasn't used to all this so she made a deal with Tinh on the preparation of dinner. One night Jane would prepare all American dishes and the next night Tinh would prepare all Vietnamese dishes. Both were excellent cooks and we were introduced to some fine Vietnamese foods. Jane and I loved the change of diet but Gery and Mary Kay had a problem learning new foods. Lori didn't have any problem adjusting to the Vietnamese dinners, but seemed to feel left out when I gave attention to Lai. All in all, the arrangement worked well. We found a house for them in Spanish Lake and they moved in before Christmas. The winter of 1975-76 was very cold with much ice and show. The Phams were not accustomed to cold weather and wished for a warmer climate. They finally sold and located in Pasadena, Texas. We visited them in their new home several times and were invited to Lai's beautiful wedding. Lai and her husband are both dentists and they have a beautiful son, Nicholas.

Several years after their move to Texas, Ninh called me on the telephone to tell us that they were now American Citizens. He was quite proud as were Jane and I. They chose American names and he is now Ray Pham, his wife Tina and his daughter Kathleen. We appreciate the relationship with this fine, hard working family and always wish them well!

***

Alan wanted something to do during his summer break from college in 1975 so we agreed to pay him a modest monthly fee for clearing some ground where we would build, including an area south of the barn. He stayed in the barn loft, drew bath water from the well or bathed in the creek and had a fun summer. While visiting some friends in Ste. Genevieve, someone drove a four wheeler around the closed gate and stole many items from our barn loft. We had a phone call early in the morning and somehow, I knew it was going to be Alan with some bad news. He was upset but the loss was not great. It just makes you anxious each time you visit a property which has been unoccupied for a week.

Construction work was slow in 1977 and Joe and Bob were between jobs. They agreed to build our house while staying in the barn during the week and driving home on weekends. They did a great job and constructed the house according to our plans. We were indebted to both my brothers for their skill and willingness to help. I paid them what they would have received in the trade.

The house was now completed but I wouldn't retire early until January 1979. Jane's sister Catherine and her husband were anxious to move from Jennings and locate in the Farmington area. We offered them our property rent free for a year or until they found a house in Farmington. This would provide some help to them and also have our home occupied in our absence. We could still go down on week ends and stay in or little loft apartment.

Electric was not available while Joe and Bob were building the house so I purchased a gas generator for their use and our future needs. Now that the house was built and would be occupied, Union Electric agreed to run electric the half mile to our house. They cleared a right of way along the edge of our property and cut the large oak trees into eight foot lengths. Gery knew that Jane always wanted a split rail fence, so he split 200 rails and built a fence around the yard. Quite a feat and we were pleased and thankful for his generous effort!

Boo had been diagnosed with cancer and treatment was not working. They removed his spleen but the cancer continued to take his life. Boo had malaria while in New Guinea and we always felt that this had somehow contributed to his weakened resistance to the various treatments prescribed.

***

The area served by The North Side Bank (now Charter Bank of Jennings) was changing with many of our good old families moving elsewhere. In recognizing this change, I became very aware of the open exposure of all of our teller's windows and decided to have bullet proof windows installed at each station. My friend Bo was now a senior officer at the main Charter Bank in Kansas City, and he objected to the installation, fearing that it would take away some of the beauty of the bank interior. We ordered the windows, over his objection, and had the supporting stanchions installed. It would be a wait of several weeks before the glass would be delivered and installed. My concern for the safety of our tellers intensified and I, somehow, had a bad feeling of on impending problem. I checked with our head teller to learn how much cash each teller had in their window. It was too much! I had them keep no more than $10,000 and place any overage in their lockers in the main vault.

Several days later, while I was writing notes in preparation for a reply to a recent bank examination, I heard a loud crash in the lobby. I jumped up to see what happened but was stopped by my secretary as she whispered, "Stay back, it's a robbery and they are holding a customer hostage with a gun to his neck!" I sounded the silent alarm, dialed the police, went to the window and saw an automobile parked directly in front of the bank. I wrote down the license number, make of the auto, color and description. The bank robbers ran to the car and nearly left one of their group as the car sped out from the curb. He screamed at them, they stopped, he jumped in and they made their escape. I could not identify any of the party, except that they were all black! One of our bank customers, who was delivering papers in Walnut Park, saw this auto with five or six black occupants. They parked the auto and quickly entered another while carrying some bags. He thought it was strange so he wrote down the license number and description of the auto they entered. This information, together with my information, enabled the FBI to capture the robbers the same night, but the money was already gone.

Fortunately, with our reduced tellers' cash, we lost only $8000. It could have been much worse! I testified against the robbers and my notes were taken as evidence to link the two automobiles together during the robbery. All principals were convicted and sentenced! Had the bullet proof window not been ordered, I think most of our tellers would have quit!

Incidents seem to be increasing! We were surprised when someone used the men's room on the lower level, took our Vice

Presidents hat and defecated in it! Yes, our neighborhood was changing!

While working at my desk in my office one morning, two young men charged past my secretary and slammed a check on my desk. The larger of the two, about 6 feet tall, spoke, or rather shouted, "The tellers wouldn't cash my check and I'm demanding that you cash it!" I looked at the check, noting that it was on insurance claim check made out to two people. In checking the endorsement, it was obvious that the same person signed both names. I told the young man to have the other party come in to sign the check and we would be willing to cash the check!" He said, "You didn't hear me mister, I'm demanding that you cash this check!" I told him he could demand all he wanted but until it was properly endorsed I would not cash it. He then said if I didn't, he would kill me and then picked up an office chair and threw it across the desk at me. I lunged at him and they both ran and separated. I caught up with the larger one and he turned and raised his arms to swing at me. I told him if he swung at me I was going to take him a part! He ran, thank the Lord! That old hot blooded farm and wartime background could be damaging to my health! I caught the other young man as he was leaving the parking lot in his car.

The police arrived as I stopped his car. He was terrified! He swore that he only agreed to drive his friend to the bank, and knew nothing of the endorsement being forged. After obtaining the name and address of his friend, we released him. I then swore out a warrant for his friend's arrest. About an hour later the chief of police called to tell me that they picked up the individual about a half mile from the bank. He was on his way back to the bank with his gun! Banking was becoming dangerous! Later, at the pleading of the individual's father, I agreed to drop the charges provided that his son would seek mental help.

***

Boo's battle with cancer was taking its toll and his health was declining rapidly. Ferd, Harry Davis and I visited Boo at his home and while we were talking, he staggered and began to fall. Harry caught him but Boo was embarrassed. We tried to act as though we didn't notice his condition, but it never worked. Shortly thereafter, Boo was hospitalized at Barnes Hospital. He would never return!

The day before he died, Sis, Mary and I went to see him. They would only allow one at a time to enter his intensive care room. When I went in I was shocked and saddened at his condition. The IV needles couldn't stay in his arms as his flesh was just pulling apart. I didn't want to, but started to cry! Boo said, "What's the matter, Ray?" I told him it was hard to see him like this and there was nothing I could do to help! We had always gone the extra mile to help each other. Boo said, "It's alright Ray, I'm OK!" After I left his room they rushed into his room to add more equipment. I questioned his doctor and he told me that Boo had a good chance to make it. I knew he was lying! The next day Boo died. It was April 6, 1976. Later when I paid the bills for Boo's last days, I could see what they did. They knew there was no chance of his surviving more than a few days so we were billed for a number of last items, equipment, *plus* bills from two doctors, whom we never heard of, for last minute consulting fees of $200 each! When asked for Boo's personal items to be returned to the family, we learned that they had lost Boo's watch! My opinion of Barnes Hospital was as low as it could get and hope I, or any of our family ever goes there again!

Boo's wife was having health problems of her own and it was a very difficult time for his family and for all of us. In the years to come I would experience the loss of most of my family. A bit of me died with every one!

**

John had made good friends with a German who had served as a medic during World War II. His name was Joe Kreinhoefner and a gentle, considerate man. He visited us several times and considered John as a brother. Joe had shrapnel wounds with some parts of the metal still imbedded in his body. While walking to Mass in his home town in Germany, the shrapnel apparently moved causing his death. It was on February 1, 1987. We will always remember Joe and his gentle nature.

Time moved on with Rita and Jean solidly becoming Californians, John working in the heating and cooling industry, Alan working in Columbia while finishing college in 1977, Paul in the Navy, Gery was selling insurance, and Mary Kay and Lori still in school. All had varied work experiences before settling on their careers. Alan and Paul had worked together on construction of a department store, Paul as Santa Claus one Christmas, a stint at Sambo's restaurant and Lombardo's Italian restaurant. Alan got his degree in Forestry from Mizzou in December 1978.

Since the Hidden Lake building project was a monetary and mental drain on me, I offered to sell my corporation (RAJA) to Don Young for $1. I had paid in capital of $30,000 and RAJA had about $80,000 in profit from sales and homes to be sold. Approximately $10,000 was in RAJA's bank account. I also had a personal loan of about $30,000 secured by my bank stock. Don didn't have any cash money but did have equity in six rental homes in Las Lomas and Florissant subdivisions. We estimated his equity to be about $20,000 in the six homes so he took $10,000 from RAJA's checking account and transferred title to his six rentals. I now became a landlord and that worried me also. I was anxious to pay my personal loan and retrieve my bank stock. I paid the $10,000 to principal, put the six houses up for sale and eventually retired my personal loan and retrieved my bank stock.

The net experience resulted in my loss of the $30,000 capital I had paid into RAJA and a lot of experience enabling me to continue my by-line of "Buy High and Sell Low." Don and I remained good friends. He eventually got out of Hidden Lake with a little money, built a subdivision in Warrenton, Missouri, along with apartments and a motel. He retired to Tampa, Florida, where he died after losing both legs due to an illness. Jane and I visited Don and his wife, Virginia, several times before his death.

***

The banking scene was changing rapidly and the regulatory bank examiners were often required to place more emphasis on compliance rather than loan quality. Compliance forms documenting interest rate disclosures, loan application to verify that you were not discriminating against anyone and a host of other documentations had to be accurately recorded and maintained. Since new compliance regulations were being implemented on a steady basis, I maintained that every bank was in violation of *something* but they didn't know it!

We had obtained Trust Powers for the bank and the six or seven trust accounts were now also my responsibility. When two trust examiners from the State Division of Finance came to my office and announced that they would be there for a week to examine my few accounts, I could hardly believe it. I asked what they would do for a whole week, when the entire portfolio could be examined and evaluated by *one* person in no more that two days. One of the examiners was a young woman who apparently wanted to make a name for herself. When the week was over, they had scrutinized every piece of correspondence in our trust portfolio. When I later received the commissioner's report, I clarified her comments with a scathing letter. The following year the same young woman conducted a regular exam at the bank and told me that the letter I had written to the Commissioner on her trust exam was awfully strong. I just smiled and said, "You should have seen the first letter I wrote and decided not to send that!"

I loved banking and our customers but the changing regulatory environment was really getting to me. I looked forward to an early retirement and felt we could make it alright on our property in Farmington. I decided to retire on January 1, 1979 and gave my notice to that effect.

Jane's sister and brother-in-law had been occupying our house at the farm but had since purchased a nice home in Farmington. The house would be vacant and ready to occupy at any time.

Mary Kay had graduated and was now working for the Bank of Overland. Jane wanted Lori to start her new school year in Farmington in the fall of 1978, so it was important that we move soon so that everyone would be settled. We sold our home in Hidden Lake at a bargain price to some friends and I rented an apartment close to Bank of Overland where Mary Kay and I would reside until my retirement in January 1979. We moved to Farmington in June 1978, or rather Jane and Lori moved to the farm, and I would be there on weekends and vacation.

I did all the cooking for Mary Kay and myself at our apartment in Overland. We had a six month lease. I don't think Mary Kay was impressed with my menu or my cooking but she only grinned and didn't complain. I learned many ways to prepare meat loaf and we ate a lot of spaghetti, bacon, eggs, beans and hamburgers.

Gery rented an apartment and continued selling insurance. Paul would later share housing with Gery when he returned from his six year enlistment in the Navy. Gery eventually moved into construction and his natural abilities became quite evident. His final change was a good move into real estate appraisal which has become his permanent occupation.

***

I retired from The North Side Bank of Jennings on the first Monday in January 1979. Since I was a member of the Board of Directors, they wanted me to continue in that capacity. I was pleased since I would then collect a director's monthly fee of $200. During the board meeting they asked me to step outside since they had a surprise for me. A pickup truck, with side cattle panels, was parked on the lot with it's cargo, a young black angus steer, who was about to go berserk! He was standing on his hind legs trying to break down the side panels to escape. They were to deliver the steer to Farmington! It was a generous and thoughtful retirement gift but the purchase of same was ill advised. Bo had contacted a correspondent banker from the Stockyards in Illinois and he arranged the purchase of a steer that had never been weaned from his mother. He was wild!

I called Jane at the farm to tell her that a steer was being delivered and since I had only twenty acres fenced at that time, she and Lori should be sure to have them put the steer in the fenced area. I would be down later that day when the board meeting and final departure procedures were complete. That night it snowed! It was dark when I reached the farm and couldn't see the steer anywhere. There was nothing to do but wait until morning to find him. In the morning I found his track in the snow and saw where he broke through the fence. I finally saw the steer on the other side of the lake but when I tried to approach him with some hay and grain, he bounded off like a wild deer. I could no longer find his track in the woods where only a tracing of the snow remained. I then placed hay at several places, hoping he would settle down, find something to eat and allow me to approach him. It didn't happen!

The next morning was not successful and I called Walter Neiter, a friend who built our lake and also owned a nice herd of cattle on his farm near Ste. Genevieve. Walter told me we would never be able to approach the steer since it was not weaned and would be completely wild and frightened. He suggested going horse back to herd or drive the animal back to the fenced area. I knew of no one to do that and time was running out for the steer!

Since my sister Mary and her husband Harry lived only a half mile from us, I asked Harry to help me. I had sold 20 acres of my original purchase to my brother Bob and he sold one acre to Harry and Mary and helped them build their home there. Harry suggested I get more help so I talked to 'Moon' McMillan, my neighbor, who adjoined our property on the south. He also would help. I loaded my 30.06 Mauser and met Harry and Moon on Knob Lick Road. We now knew that it would be necessary to kill the animal or risk losing him once he crossed the road! I handed the rifle to Harry. He said, no way would he be able to shoot the steer! Moon answered my plea the same way. I had to do it!

We spread out on the 40 acres between our property and Knob Lick Road. After about an hour I saw some tracks in the leaves and snow and shortly thereafter spotted the steer on a hillside about 100 yards away. He saw me and started to run. I whistled and he stopped and looked directly at me. I had a scope on my rifle and fired a round right between his eyes! He dropped like a rock! I had feared wounding him but that didn't happen! I went back to our barn, installed a three point boom on the tractor and returned. Harry, Moon and I tied the legs of the steer, hoisted him with the boom and took him to the barn. There we dressed and skinned him. I called my friend, Walter Neiter, and told him that we had the steer dressed and skinned. Walter had a cooler in his basement and had all the equipment for processing beef. He told me to bring the steer over and we would hang it in his cooler to age for a week or so. I told him we would be over the next day. It began to snow hard!

We wrapped the steer carcass in a tarp and placed it in the bed of my pickup truck. Since it was well below freezing there was no risk of spoilage. The next morning we awoke to about ten inches of snow and bitter cold. I put chains on the truck and started out. On the road to Walter's farm, about ten miles from our house, I was stopped by a snow drift of more than three feet blocking the road. Several other trucks were stalled there also. We all worked together to get through the drift and I finally made it, only to find the road impassable farther on. I found a side road to return to the farm where we waited for nearly a week to deliver our frozen beef. We finally managed to reach Walter's farm, hung the beef to 'age.' I think it was already aged! The following week Walter and I ground the entire steer into hamburger! A 500 pound steer makes a lot of hamburger!

***

Our adventuresome daughter, Mary Kay worked at ferrying automobiles to California and then signed up for a season at Yellowstone National Park Inn in Montana. In the meanwhile she contributed to our grey hair by participating in steer riding and bronco riding at a rodeo. Watching her participate in the rodeo events was too much for loving parents! We said a grateful prayer when she found other activities. When Mary Kay completed her agreement at Yellowstone National Park she came home and was employed by "Your Man Tours," a travel agency. The following year she signed up for a season at Glacier National Park in Montana. Our friend Dr. Donald Callahan and I flew his plane to Kalispell and visited Mary Kay at East Glacier Lodge, where she was employed.

After leaving East Glacier Lodge, Mary Kay rented an apartment in St. Paul, Minnesota while she worked for Burlington Northern Credit Union. We visited her mouse infested quarters in St. Paul and agreed to move her meager possessions back to Missouri. It was hard to keep up with Mary Kay! In St. Louis, she worked for the St. Louis Credit Union and then Western Union for thirteen years. Finally, at age 32, Mary returned to school, obtained a degree in accounting, passed her exam for CPA and found her permanent employment (we hope) as an auditor for Anheuser Bush.

In the spring of 1979, Alan and a friend toured the country seeking employment in their field of forestry. Their search brought them to Montana where Alan found the beauty of the mountains and Glacier National Park. He found employment with Champion International and chose Kalispell as his base.

We wanted to be self sufficient on our property in Farmington, so we designed our house to be heated by a wood burning stove (we had plenty of wood), and constructed a 'root cellar' to store canned fruit and vegetables from our garden.

We excavated an area of 8 feet by 20 feet, poured reinforced concrete walls and floors and poured an 8 inch reinforced ceiling. It was my intention to just cover this with earth, but my brother Bob suggested that we build a wood shed on the top since the floor of concrete was already there. He could get some material from a wrecked mansard roof which would work, with some modifications, for the roof trusses. Bob and I built shelves along one wall for storing canned goods. One large freezer was placed on the other wall. The trusses from the mansard roof provided an 18 inch overhang on both sides and with the soffet uncovered provided cross ventilation and air to keep the firewood dry. Bob was a master at thinking things through and, as I would rush into a project, Bob would say, "Wait a minute, let's think about this!" I will always be indebted to Bob and rarely does a day pass that I do not think of him and all that we did together. While I loved him as my brother, he also was the best friend I ever had!

We found the remains of an old cabin in a cedar grove on the back 40. All that remained of the cabin was the stone foundation and stone hearth. The evidence of an old road about 100 feet in front of the cabin could still be seen. I wanted to know something of that cabin and why it was built there. At one time there must have been a spring in the cedar grove about 20 feet from the cabin. I learned that the road was the old wagon road, known as the 'Ridge Road' which connected Farmington to Knob Lick. We researched the Abstract for our property and found that it was part of a section (620 acres) owned by one party who had three slaves. His will granted freedom to the three slaves and gave them a life estate to remain on this property. We found the remains of another dwelling on the south side of our lake. We often wondered if these sites were the original location of homes the slaves built after their freedom.

We removed the stones from the foundation in the back forty and used them for the foundation of our smoke house. I had plans for the type of smoke house which was often used in the 1800's. This plan called for the fire pit to be outside the smoke house, with the smoke piped underground to come up in the center of the smoke house. I formed the fire pit and poured concrete walls and ceiling with a small smoke stack through the ceiling. This fire pit was built about six feet behind the smoke house. We completed the smoke house which was 4 feet wide, 8 feet deep and 8 feet high with a hip roof open at both ends. Joe and I split oak shingles for the roof of this building and also for a little well house I built over the well. When we were ready to smoke our cured hams, shoulders and bacons, we would build a hickory fire in the pit while keeping the smoke stack open. When the fire pit had a good bed of coals, I would place green hickory on the coals and cover the stack, thereby forcing smoke through the pipe to the floor of the smoke house. It worked great!

We initially raised our own hogs and, with the help of Bob, Joe, Ferd and Harry, killed, scalded, scraped and butchered them. I used Pop's recipe for curing solution for up to six weeks for the hams and shoulders but only about ten days for the bacons. We then washed them in cold water and smoked them for about 48 hours. This produced some of the best bacon and hams we could hope for. One of our good friends asked us to cure some bacon for him and he always reminded us of how good they were.

We had our friend, Walter Neiter, clear sixteen acres on the ridge on the back 40 and also several acres below the lake. This area was along our wet weather creek, had good soil and became the area for our large garden of sweet corn, melons, and cucumbers. We also had a small garden by the barn on which we grew about 200 tomatoes, string beans and peppers. We then planted a number of fruit trees including peaches, apricots, nectarines, apples and pears. The deer and wild life loved all of our efforts.

***

Alan told us that he and Mary Klein had set a date of July 20, 1979, to be married, after which they would make their home in Kalispell, Montana. The wedding would be at the Catholic Church in Ste. Genevieve and reception to follow. Rev James Bierster, a classmate of Alan's at St. Henry's Seminary would say the Mass. Jane's mom and dad came down to spend the night with us before the wedding so that we could all drive together to Ste. Genevieve. It was a beautiful wedding. On the way back to Farmington, Jane's dad's Chrysler developed engine trouble and nearly stalled which upset John very much. He complained of it being too warm which was not evident to us. We didn't realize he had a heart problem which would later take his life. On August 9, 1979, we received a call from Bud Gillespie (Jane's brother-in-law) that John had died suddenly of a heart attack. It was very hot with a heat warning when John decided to mow their lawn at their home in Jennings. He completed the lawn, sat down on a lawn chair, collapsed and died. It was quite a shock for all of us and a great concern for Catherine (Jane's mom).

Alan bought a pickup truck and I bought a camper shell for him. He and Mary loaded all their possessions and moved to Kalispell. We now had children in California and Montana. We would later add another state as John and his family moved to Minnesota.

We purchased a 1979 Ford Fiesta, a tiny car which proved to be quite comfortable and provided excellent gas mileage.

We decided to take a trip to California to see Rita and Jean early in 1980. It was a fun trip. We enjoyed driving the little car and got up to 40 miles to the gallon. It was great visiting with Rita and Jean.

John was looking for some acreage in the Farmington area and we found sixteen acres northeast of our farm. John and Sue built their home and moved in on November 11, 1980.

Paul completed his six year enlistment in the Navy, returned home in February, 1980 and was employed by Coherent Radiation. After one year, Paul left Coherent Radiation and was employed by The North Side Bank where he met and fell in love with a sweet girl named Barbara Gentile. They were married on October 10, 1981.

***

In the fall of 1981, Lee Walker, Vice President of the Charter Corporation and a good friend, called to arrange a visit with me at the farm. Charter had purchased The North Side Bank, Bank of Overland, Webster Groves Trust and Bank of Ladue, all in the St. Louis County area. Lee asked me if I would be interested in taking over the CEO position at Webster Groves Trust since they wanted to change top management there. I was restless with my "early retirement plan" and was pleased to learn of the offer.

Gordon Wells, Chairman and CEO of Charter, together with some members of his staff, flew down to attend our Board of Directors meeting at North Side which was followed by our Directors Christmas party. I was asked to return to Kansas City with them to work out the arrangement and agreements for my acceptance of the Webster Groves position. Unfortunately, a bitter Missouri winter storm, with ice and snow, prevented our flight to Kansas City. We stayed at a motel in St. Louis and when the weather did not improve the next day, we agreed to meet at the regular Board of Directors meeting at Webster Groves Trust the first week of January when I would be elected Chairman and CEO.

On the day of the Board meeting, Gordon and Lee Walker met with me for lunch since the meeting would start at 2 p.m. After lunch we drove around the Webster Groves area so that I could see the site which was previously purchased for a facility for the bank. I was not impressed with the location and told them so! Gordon seemed anxious about introducing me to the board since I only knew two of the members. He asked me, "Ray, you're not going to tell the Board that you are from Farmington, are you?" I was surprised at this question and answered, "Of course not, Gordon, I'm going to tell them that I'm from Knob Lick," a little spot south of Farmington! He seemed shocked, so I added, "Gordon, if you expect me to be anything other than who I am, you may as well turn the car around now. I will have no problem with the board and I am a good banker!" He said he wasn't worried about that at all and it was just a comment.

The Board of Directors was made up of some very fine men who became good friends. I had agreed to spend at least five years with the bank. During the five years I met many wonderful people in the area, enjoyed the challenge and was proud of our accomplishments!

I rented an apartment in Webster Groves for the first year of my employment. Gery stayed with me while working in the St. Louis area. Jane remained at the farm and joined us in Webster Groves on Wednesday and Thursday. I spent the weekends at the farm and returned to the bank on Monday morning. This meant some highway driving for both of us, but it seemed to work out well.

When my one year lease was up, we bought a split level house in Shrewsbury and continued the weekend arrangements to the farm. Gery had rented a home more central to his work so I had a large house by myself except when Jane stayed over. Paul and Barb now had two children, Tony and Stephanie. They needed larger quarters so I asked them to share our home in Shrewsbury. The arrangement worked out well and I no longer had to endure my cooking! Barb is an excellent cook!

Lori married Darrin Ferguson on August 12, 1983. Three children were born of that marriage, Amanda, Coty and Bobby. Jean married Mike Delaney in November the same year. Since we had bought a small Champion motor home, we invited Mary Kay to join us for the trip to Texas for Jean's wedding. The motor home was underpowered with a six cylinder Ford engine. When we returned from Texas we traded the Champion for a 25-foot Rockwood motor home with a Ford 460 engine. This was a comfortable RV. The 460 engine was fond of gas and provided about nine miles per gallon. Gery married Joyce Capstick on March 2, 1984. Their three children are Samantha Ann, Kristan Lee, and Alicia Joy.

***

The years working under the Charter Bank ownership were enjoyable. Charter had many fine people in their organization and I had a free reign at Webster. Many good bankers were represented in the banks under the Charter banner when Boatmen's Bank bought out the Charter Corporation. Banking, as I knew it, would soon disappear. While there were a number of fine people in the Boatmen's organization, there were some really arrogant and pompous jerks. I looked forward to the completion of my five year guarantee.

I would be eligible for retirement at age 60 which would occur on December 27, 1987. Retirement under the Charter plan fell through in the fall of 1987, under which I would have received an annual cost of living adjustment of 2 percent. Since Boatmen's did not have the cost of living adjustment in their plan, it would be lost to me. Had I been able to retire under Charter my retirement would now be 40 percent greater!

***

My World War II Merchant Marine sailing buddy, DeWayne Schwanke, owned an Avion travel trailer and belonged to the Avion travel club. He suggested that we buy an Avion and travel together when I retired. This would mean that we would have to purchase a tow vehicle, buy an Avion and sell the Rockwood motor home. We did it! Of course, I lost money on the 1984 Rockwood, but found a like new, 30-foot Avion for a good price, which was delivered to us at Farmington by the seller. We then ordered a new one ton Ford cargo van with a 460 engine and my brother Joe finished the cargo interior so that the van alone could be self sufficient. He built in storage boxes which could be converted to a bed, a chuck wagon type box accessible from the two rear cargo doors and fully insulated and paneled the interior. We had Joe do all of this since we planned a trip to Alaska after retirement and did not want to pull a 30-foot trailer. Joe did an excellent job!

We made plans with the Schwanke's to take our first trip to the Baja in Mexico. The site we chose was about 800 miles south of the border in the village of Mulege. We acquired boxes of stuffed animals, toys, candy, shoes and clothing to be given to the Mexican children, and loaded our cargo van with the items.

DO TELL - II

    I retired from the bank the first week of January, 1987, and a few days later, hitched up the Avion, put skid chains on the van and started out our snow and ice covered lane. We needed the chains to reach the cleared highway. I wouldn't be brave or foolish enough to do that now! It was agreed that we meet the Schwanke's in Yuma, Arizona, at the residence of their relatives and travel together into Mexico. I had never towed anything this large before and, even though we had all the proper equipment, the adrenalin pumped vigorously through our veins on the first few days. After that we considered ourselves to be old pros!

    We arrived in Yuma without mishap and met DeWayne and Milly at the agreed spot. The next day we shopped for groceries and supplies for our trip into Mexico. Both DeWayne and I had our 14-foot aluminum fishing boats on the top of our tow vehicles and carried our outboard motors in the tow vehicles. We agreed to stop overnight somewhere in California, just north of the Mexican border.

    DeWayne was in the lead and said he had a relative on some acreage in that area and we could park our rigs there overnight. We followed him down some narrow roads until we both agreed that he was lost and couldn't find the relative's place. After much inexperienced maneuvering I finally got our rig turned around and we retraced our route to the highway. We then selected a commercial campground which was located in a pretty valley.

    In checking in, the owner told us to select a site in the valley and then come up and register. I followed DeWayne. The camping sites were located around a cul-de-sac and bordered on a small canyon. I watched DeWayne pull around the cul-de-sac and it looked easy, so I followed. I didn't want to get too close to the canyon so I turned too short. The center of the cul-de-sac was planted in shrubs with a small palm tree in the center. When I seemed to hang up on something, I heard Milly screaming for us to stop! There was a water hydrant near the palm tree which I had broken off with the front tire of the tandem axel of the trailer! Water was shooting high in the air, the tire was ruptured and the broken hydrant wedged between the tandem wheels! DeWayne quickly unhitched his rig and offered to hook on the rear of our Avion and pull me back off the hydrant. When he started to pull, the bumper of the Avion pulled off! We then called a wrecker! After several unsuccessful attempts by the wrecker, a neighbor came down and offered the use of an old axel which could be inserted into the Avion frame to provide a place to which the tow truck could attach. This worked, except for the fact that when he raised the trailer, all of the rivets popped out on the left side! We placed something under the wheels to clear the hydrant and were finally freed. In the meanwhile Jane and Milly had gone to the office to ask them to turn the water off to the campground. There was no way to turn it off! It was supplied by a large tank on the hill and would drain the tank dry! The under panel of our Avion was ripped, two tires were ruptured and I wanted to push the Avion in the canyon! My nerves were not too good! We asked the tow truck driver where we could get our bumper reattached and buy two new tires. He agreed to meet us at his station the next morning where he repaired the bumper and replaced the tires. This trip was not starting out very well! I gave the park owner my address and the name of our insurance company, and then wrote to our agent to explain what I did. We left the campground with a good feeling for the owners but with a very unhappy Mexican employee who had to deal with the broken pipes and water problem!

We crossed the border into Mexico and headed south with our destination somewhere on the Baja Peninsula. We heard many horror stories of travel in Mexico but met only fine people who always seemed anxious to help. We purchased Mexican auto insurance and bought Mexican fishing licenses. We were instructed to take the original title to our van, boat and trailer, but I made copies instead and left the originals at home. This would later cause a bit of tension when we started back to the states. I'll describe that later.

About 700 or 800 miles south of the border we reached the little town named Mulege. It was located on a fresh water stream which entered the Gulf of California about one mile from a pretty campground. We rented a site, launched our boat and moored it in the stream only a short distance from our campsite. At high tide we could motor to the ocean and fish for cabria, a great tasting type of sea bass, which were easily caught while fishing 80 to 100 feet deep. Of course, there were other fish to be caught but we preferred the cabria. We explored the area, met some fellow Americans and also some English speaking Mexicans. Before leaving home, we collected many toys, clothes, shoes and candy to give to the children. We asked the campground owner where we could try to distribute the toys and clothes. He suggested an area away from Mulege and gave us directions. We followed a dirt road into the boonies and finally came to some sort of encampment which consisted of tar-paper shacks, small thatched lean-to dwellings and old cars. We asked three Mexican men where we could find the children since we had gifts for them. We used our little book to translate English to Spanish. They didn't understand a word we said!

We saw a young boy sitting on a wood fence behind the men, so I took a toy truck from the van and approached the men and boy, indicating the toy as a gift. They then understood as we presented the toy truck to the boy, and women and children seemed to appear from everywhere. DeWayne and Milly Schwanke were with us and together we distributed most of the clothing and toys and much of the candy. The women and children were very polite and would take but one item until we urged them to take more. Shoes were a popular item and we wished we had collected more before leaving home, although we had little room for more of anything in the van.

We purchased fresh sea scallops from the fishermen and were fascinated to see how they improvised their diving equipment to collect the scallops. Never again shall we enjoy better sea food or more delightful happy people! We gathered our own clams from the sea in shallow water. It took only a short while to fill a five gallon bucket with tasty clams. DeWayne learned to make a great margarita following the directions of a Mexican in town. We were cautioned and warned about the water and food, but we ate where other Americans recommended and had no problems. One of our favorite places was a thatched restaurant on the sea shore where we bought complete lobster dinners for about $4 including our drinks.

On Valentines Day we had dinner at a restaurant on a hill overlooking the ocean. The place was recommended by an artist we met in Mulege. When we mentioned his name, the owner insisted on furnishing us with free margaritas. It turned into a lively evening with dancing to a great mariachi band. DeWayne wanted the band to play the song, "Jose Cuervo, You are a Friend of Mine," and he called our waiter over instructing him to make the request to the band. The message was misunderstood and the waiter served Jose Cuervo tequila to the entire band and charged it to DeWayne. The process was repeated throughout the evening and the band really got 'stoned!' The more they drank, the better they played and we found ourselves dancing with Mexican senoritas and the girls with Mexican men. We had a great time! Never did hear "Jose Cuervo, You are a Friend of Mine"! We learned the following morning (Sunday) a great breakfast would be served and the Mariachi Band would be there. We decided to attend after we went to church. We saw a number of the Mariachi band on the way to the restaurant but they were either sitting on the side of the road or lying by some rocks with some serious hangovers! They never made it to the breakfast but the food was great with complimentary 'Bloody Mary's' served by the owner. DeWayne's bill for the dinner, all the tequila for the band and their drinks with tips was $36 American. What a night!

DeWayne wanted to take our 14-foot boats to a small island in the Gulf of California to do some fishing for yellowtail or trigger fish. It looked a long way out but we agreed to go. About three miles into the ocean, Jane asked if there were whales in these waters. I told her this was the calving ground for whales and she pointed off our stern on the port side. A pod of Orcas (killer whales) were about 50 yards from our boat. I assured Jane that they would not bother us but she felt insecure. They passed very close as I prayed they would not consider our little boat a toy and bump us around. They passed by without incident. We reached the island, the water was beautiful and we watched many different fish swimming among the coral. It was a long trip and we were glad to return to our little campsite and trailer on the river.

DeWayne wanted to take a ferry across the Gulf of California to Guaymas, Mexico, to see that part of Mexico and find better roads for our return north. I rode with DeWayne in his truck to Santa Rosalita to make reservations for the ferry. We needed the exact measurements of the tow vehicle and trailer to obtain a ticket. DeWayne had his truck for measurements and convinced the officer about the length of his Avion and obtained the ticket. Since I had neither my van nor trailer the officer refused. I slipped $20 into his palm and got the ticket. Now we had to prove ownership to another officer in a separate building. DeWayne presented his original titles and received permission. My copies were not accepted. Another $20 got my permission and my ferry ticket. It was a long overnight ferry boat ride, with our sleeping on the deck with some Mexicans, but we arrived at Guaymas OK. We spent a week in Guaymas and finally headed north to the good old USA.

We agreed with the Schwankes before taking our separate routes home that we would tour Alaska the summer of 1987. We would agree on dates and make reservations on the Alaskan Ferry from Prince Rupert, British Columbia, Canada to Skagway, Alaska.

When we got back to Farmington, we equipped the van for living arrangements and my brother Joe built a chuck wagon type unit in the back part of the van for cooking supplies, utensils and propane stove with tank. We planned to pull the Avion to Kalispell, Montana, visit Alan and Mary, leave the Avion at their place and drive the van the rest of the trip. It worked out really well and it turned out to be another of our great travel experiences. We met a very nice Canadian couple from Calgary while we were in Mexico and they urged us to visit them on our way to Alaska and take in the Calgary Stampede. We agreed to do so and contacted them when we reached home. They obtained great seats for the stampede since they were on the stampede committee. They also took us on a tour of Calgary and the surrounding area as they were preparing for the Olympics that summer. We very much enjoyed our visit with these fine folks.

We visited Banff and Jasper then took the Yellowhead highway to Prince Rupert to board the ferry for the Inland Passage to Skagway. From Skagway we began our great tour of Alaska to Valdez, Anchorage, the Homer Spit, Denali, Fairbanks and back to the lowers states by way of the Okanagan Valley, then to Kalispell where we met Jean and her husband on Labor Day. We received sad news when we reached Kalispell since Loretta, Ferd's wife, had died suddenly on August 24, 1987. It was a long trip but a most enjoyable one. Jane wanted to do it again and I reluctantly agreed provided I could take my 14-foot boat. We finally made that second trip in 1995. I will describe that trip later.

DeWayne Schwanke called us in 1988 to describe property in Bowling Green, Florida, which had been purchased by a group from the Avion Travel Club and being developed into a first class camping resort. He and Milly were joining the group and contracted for the purchase of an RV lot there. He wanted to know if we would be interested in purchasing a lot (not yet developed) also. We decided to wait. In 1989 we drove our car to Bowling Green to look at the development and decided to buy a lot. The RV Park, called Avion Palms was very well done and we enjoyed our winters there for several years.

***

Much of John's work was in St. Louis which required a long commute, and he started thinking of some changes. Sue was operating a stitchery shop from their home which was proving to be time consuming and not too profitable. John wanted to move to Minnesota and finally convinced Sue that it was the thing to do. They sold their property in Farmington and bought a lot on Fish Trap Lake near Cushing, Minnesota, on the opposite shore where DeWayne and Milly lived.

On May 2, 1990, I towed a small travel trailer to their lot on the lake. John would first build a two car detached garage and the trailer and garage would be their living quarters until their home was finished in October 1990. Glad the marriage survived those living conditions! It speaks well for perseverance and patience.

Mary Kay married Donn Finkenkeller on May 19, 1990. Our 'wild child' now a married woman! Would she settle down now and give our few remaining gray hairs a rest? I doubt it!

Dick Heaton, an Avion RV friend from the state of Washington invited us to join him at Port Angeles on the Olympic peninsula to fish the Straits of Juan de Fuca for salmon. He had his own boat in a marina there. It was something I always wanted to do. We began the trip with our 1986 Ford van but developed engine problems and left the trailer in New Mexico at the St. Bonaventure Indian Mission RV Park, drove back home and purchased a 1990 Ford, extended cab diesel pickup truck. It was a great vehicle. We finally arrived (a bit late) at the RV park in Port Angeles and enjoyed several weeks fishing with Dick Heaton for salmon. We repeated the trip the following year to find that the salmon were not as plentiful and more restrictions were being applied. We loved the northwest and toured much of the Olympic Peninsula and the West Coast.

***

In January of 1991, the Pastor of our Catholic Church in Florida made an urgent appeal for help to the refugees from the Russian satellite countries wanting to come to the U.S. Since many were from rural areas, Jane and I discussed the possibility of building a house on our property in Farmington and provide it free to a family.

We had the necessary farm equipment for gardening. Most fields were fenced for cattle and a barn for livestock, all of which we were not fully using. It would help a needy family and also place someone on our property for years that we hoped to continue to travel with our RV. We wrote to the address of Catholic Charities in the northeast, describing our offer and to determine if there was interest. Their "thank you" reply was prompt and enthusiastic, advising us that our letter was forwarded to the St. Louis Office. We wanted to help so we asked our son Gery for assistance in contracting to build a small three bedroom house between our barn and our dwelling. We returned home from Florida in the spring of 1991 and moved quickly on construction. Gery did a fantastic job in finding the necessary contractors and crew and in coordinating the project. Since we would be providing the electric, water and all costs, we would simply extend the water line from our well and the electric service from our home.

The completed project was a cute and efficient three bedroom house with a three foot crawl space instead of a basement. We then completely furnished the dwelling with all new furniture including gas stove, refrigerator, washer and dryer. The bedrooms furnished with new beds, mattresses, all bed clothes, linens, towels, etc. The flatware, cooking utensils and dishes were mostly furnished from surplus from our house and some lamps and extra tables were gifts from friends. The house was ready for occupancy when we received our first surprise!

I called the St. Louis Office of Catholic Charities and referred to my letter outlining our offer. The director told me that he seemed to remember the letter but no longer had it; would I send him a copy? I sent him all the information together with a description of the now completed dwelling, asking him to contact me for a visit so that his office would be able to describe the offer to any potential refugee. We received no answer! My telephone calls were not returned and I was informed that the director was either out to lunch or in a meeting and could not be reached at the time of my calls. I finally was successful in getting to him and he said he now had a family interested in our offer. We set a time for a visit the next week. Jane prepared a luncheon on the date scheduled and we waited their arrival. About noon we received a phone call advising us that the folks changed their mind and would not be coming! We had no further calls from the Catholic Charities office!

As weeks and months went by with our new refugee house unoccupied, we decided to try other avenues to help someone in need. We were given the name of a group of women who helped families in the Old Mines area. We contacted them, they were excited about our offer and agreed to come visit the following week. We never heard from them again!

When the dwelling had been completed and unoccupied for a year, we decided to check out a church in the St. Louis area which assisted families from other countries. The pastor was not interested, but agreed to put a notice in the Sunday bulletin stating "Free rent and housing in country, if interested." No response! We then ran a blind ad in a St. Louis paper stating: "Wanted - a retired senior couple on limited income. Will provide a new home, in country, fully furnished with all utilities paid in exchange for occupants watching owners home and interest in owner's absence." We received three replies! I called all three - two of which were not interested but wanted to know if this was real. We visited the third party in a nice unit in St. Louis County. After introducing ourselves, they wanted to clarify something. They were not on limited income but would want to know how far this property was from the nearest golf course before they would consider our offer! We thanked them and left. Never realized this would prove to be so difficult and not believable! Our cute, new little house would remain unoccupied for over a year.

***

1992 was a very sad year as we lost so many in deaths. Jane's mother Catherine had to have a leg removed due to gangrene, which eventually led to her death on February 5, 1992. We were with her to the end, but she was only a shell of the wonderful person whom we knew and loved. She was 96 years old.

My brother, Bob, had lung surgery and was struggling to regain his health. We visited Bob and Ginny shortly before his death. He was at their home in Creve Coeur, on oxygen, and was obviously struggling. As I sat by his bed and talked to him, he said, "It seems there is something I should be doing!" I asked if I could help and he said, "No, it is something I should do!" When Bob died on February 12, 1992, a part of me died with him! While I loved all of my family, Bob was special and I loved him very much! He was also the best friend I ever had.

My brother Tom's little grandson, Brian, also lost his battle with cancer and died at the same time. Visitation was on the same day, at the same funeral home for Bob and Brian. Hearts were heavy! As we said goodbye to these special loved ones, little did we realize we would soon lose another of our family!

Shortly after Bob's death, brother Ferd visited us at the farm in Farmington and told us that his doctor had recommended surgery to remove his prostate. We were planning to return to our property in Florida for the remainder of the winter, but in learning of Ferd's upcoming surgery, we wanted to wait to be certain that the surgery was successful. We visited Ferd in the hospital following his surgery and told him we were leaving for Florida. He said he was doing fine but the surgery was much more than he expected. We left the next day for Florida. On March 13, 1992, we had a phone call that Ferd had died from a blood clot as a result of the surgery! I was crushed! Ferd seemed so full of life and energy! We rushed home for the funeral. The great family who struggled through some tough years on the old hill farm was shrinking and the pain would remain in our hearts!

We returned to Florida after Ferd's funeral, but our heavy hearts remained and we lost some of our enjoyment of Avion Palms resort. We sold our lot to DeWayne and Milly Schwanke and came home.

We spent the winter of 1992-93 in Harlingen, Texas. It was a miserable experience due to rainy, windy weather, and a crowded RV park. We scratched Texas off our list as we pulled our Avion home. I'm sure we chose the wrong winter to try the Lone-Star State but first experiences are often lasting.

***

Our refugee house was still unoccupied and we continued our efforts to find someone who could be helped. Finally, in the fall of 1993, through the help of a Baptist Church in St. Louis, we received the Mytsa family from Moldovia, Russia, consisting of Prokopy (Peter), Tatyana (Tanya) and their three children, Natasha, Serge, and baby Daniela. Since Natasha and Serge were of school age, Jane and I enrolled them in the Farmington school system and became the 'stand-ins' for parent-teacher meetings, etc. It was rolling back time for us and an interesting experience. Both students became 'A' students in spite of their limited English and we were very proud of them! My sister Mary Davis assisted the family also and took baby Daniela to get all of the required baby shots and immunization. We found a job for Peter through Jane's nephew, found him an automobile, and introduced the family to the Baptist Church in Farmington. Members of that church were very helpful in getting them established and comfortable in our community.

Tanya's sister, Dascha, and her husband Illya, with their two children, rented an apartment in Farmington and we had many nice visits with both families. We especially enjoyed Tanya with her friendly smile and helpful ways.

***

My sister, Irene (Kimler) was suffering from failing health for some time and passed away on September 23, 1993. I visited her in the intensive care unit at the hospital before her death. She was but a shell of her former self. Her death was a continuation of the sad 1992-93 years.

John and Sue, now firmly established in Minnesota, felt the effects of ever increasing taxes on lake front property and started looking for some acreage off the lakes where John could have a shop for his sheet metal working and other crafts. They found 160 acres in Motley, Minnesota, with a nice home, a large workshop and a large Quonset building. The purchase of this property has proven to be a wise move and they agree that this will always be their home.

Our Avion friends, Phil and Myrt Taylor had purchased a lot in the Foothills out of Yuma, Arizona, and urged us to check out that part of the country. We spent the winter of 1993-94 in Yuma on a lot we rented in the Foothills. The Foothills are just west of the Gila Mountain Range with beautiful sunsets, no insects, and warm weather. We liked the area and agreed to return.

When we returned from Yuma in the spring, we learned that our Moldovia families were hoping for better paying jobs (not available in the Farmington area) and were planning to re-locate closer to some friends from Moldovia, Russia, now living on the East Coast. We were sorry to see them pack all their belongings on and in their vehicle and leave. We waved goodbye and wished them well. We felt so sorry for Tanya, who cried at their departure. We continue to hear from them and learn that they are doing well. Serge returned later for a visit to tell us he enlisted in the US Air Force. He was later sent to Iraq. We keep him in our prayers.

***

We sold our Avion and bought a 32-foot Holiday Rambler from my nephew, George Musterman and later traded the Holiday Rambler for a 34-foot Pace Arrow Motor Home. It was a very nice comfortable unit, but we still had to tow a vehicle. We bought a Saturn and all the towing attachments necessary and took a trip to the state of Washington to Sprague Lake, west of Spokane, where we met Gayle and Chris Thompson and became good friends. We told them of our plans to winter in Yuma, Arizona, and suggested they consider doing the same. We would keep in touch. Our son, Alan, and his family came down to Sprague Lake from Kalispell, Montana, and spent a few days with us.

Ron and Charlene Anderson, good friends from Carson, Washington, met us at Sprague Lake. We met Ron and Charlene in Yuma and found them to be our kind of people who we appreciate and enjoy being with. Ron's brother, Gary, and his wife were also at Sprague Lake, along with Gary's father and mother-in-law. We had some of the best wall eye fishing, but the fish had a mossy taste.

From Sprague Lake we went to Porcupine Bay on Lake Roosevelt to visit some friends, Joe and Martha Cassidy. I fished the Spokane arm of Lake Roosevelt while Jane visited with Martha. We parked our motor home on the Cassidy's property during our short visit. We then drove to Kalispell to visit Alan and family over the Fourth of July, and on south by way of Minnesota to visit John. We were shocked to arrive at John and Sue's farm to learn that John had fallen from a ladder while working a job and had shattered his ankle and leg. It would be long time healing!

***

We caught up with all the necessary mowing and chores at the farm and prepared to leave in November for Yuma. We arrived in Yuma and rented the same spot we had the year before. We also decided to look for a place to buy and found a double wide with two bedrooms, two baths, and a carport on a nice lot in the foot hills. We bought the place on December 7, 1994. It had a space on the lot for an RV and had all of the necessary hook-ups to park and connect our motor home. We had great neighbors and many great friends in various parts of the Yuma area. We visited regularly with our good friends, the Andersons and Taylors and our Canadian friends, Don "PeeWee" and Shirley Peters and their friends. We were pleased to learn that Gayle and Chris Thompson had rented a lot in the Foothills area.

We started plans for landscaping our Yuma lot, adding southwest features to the exterior and stuccoing the entire dwelling. The end result was most pleasing and brought high praise and compliments from neighbors, friends and strangers. We were quite proud of the transformation!

Since we now had a permanent residence in the Foothills in Yuma, we felt we no longer needed the big motor home. When we returned home we sold the Pace Arrow motor home and bought an 8½ foot Shadow Cruiser slide-in camper for our diesel pickup. We planned to make another trip to Alaska via the Stewart-Cassier westernmost highway. With this arrangement we would be able to pull our 14-foot boat and fish the many lakes enroute. We made the trip in 1995, stopping at Ron and Charlene Andersons' in Washington.

Travelling through Wyoming, we ran into quite a change in weather. Thunderstorms, hail and cold! It was then we discovered that I forgot to pack my warm fishing jacket. When we arrived at the Anderson's and spoke of my missing jacket with warm pockets, Charlene offered to put pockets in my heavy sweatshirt. Her skills were great and the completed project was perfect! In my attempt to show my appreciation, I wrote the following poem for her.

THANKS A BUNCH CHARLENE

Let's go 'North,' my bride declared
To the land of Mid-night Sun -
And on the way we'll visit
Our friends in Washington.

We'll pack the camper lightly
But take some winter clothes
So that we'll be comfortable-
In the land of wind and snows.

While northbound in Wyoming
In sleet, we checked our list
And much to my dismay, we found
My fishing coat - we missed.

"Not to worry" bride exclaimed,
To keep you free from harm -
I've packed a heavy sweat shirt
So you'll be safe and warm-

The shirt sure helped to break the chill
In these cold and windy lands
But - alas - to my dismay, I found
No pockets for my hands!

But then our gracious northwest friends

Whom we like so well
Said, "Come on down to Carson -
And visit for a spell!
"

While there, our super friend, Charlene
With skill beyond compare
Created pockets, of which I'm proud,
For the shirt, which I now wear.

Now as I stand and face the wind
On a lake in the great Northwest
My hands are warmly tucked inside
And so - I send my best!

Jane also sends her 'thank you'
For she knows just what I'll do -
For cold hands on her body
Turned her (pink things) blue!

From our visit with Ron and Charlene, we drove north through the Okanogan Valley to Prince Rupert in British Columbia, where we picked up the Stewart Cassiar Highway. This highway winds through very remote and beautiful country and we enjoyed the scenery, the friends we met enroute, the fishing and our little campfires each night. We always wanted to see Sitka and managed to do so on this trip. We rated Sitka as the most beautiful of our many miles in Alaska!

On our return home, we stopped to visit Alan and family in Kalispell, Montana. It was a great trip of many miles and we were glad to be back at the farm.

In the spring of 1995, a couple with two young girls had asked us about our unoccupied "refugee" house. They said their home had burned and asked us to help them until they could get back on their feet. Being trusting souls, we agreed to allow them to occupy the house. We would offer the house furnished which would also include electric, water and a full 300 gallon propane gas tank. They would only need to keep the gas tank filled. Since all appliances plus water heater and heating were gas, we had only a very modest electric bill while wintering in Yuma. That winter we were shocked to find our electric bill more than tripled - something wasn't right. Our tenants proved very disappointing. When we returned home in the spring of 1996 we found one of our Anderson windows broken in our home where someone had thrown a large mud ball. The half mile lane to our house was in bad repair due to heavy truck usage and no repairs made. We learned the cause of our high electric bills. In order to avoid replacing propane gas, they resorted to heating the house with electric space heaters.

After furnishing a house with all utilities free, we found it cost us an additional $1000 for road and window repairs and excessive electricity. So much for trusting folks! We would be more cautious in the future. We asked our free tenants to move and our 'refugee' house would remain vacant!

We took our pick up truck with the slide-in camper to Yuma that fall and decided we no longer would use it enough to justify keeping same. We offered to sell it to our friend Don "Pee Wee" Peters and agreed to deliver the rig to Fernie, B.C., Canada, the summer of 1996. Pee Wee bought the camper and we delivered it as agreed, but sadly, Pee Wee had few opportunities to enjoy it. He developed a lung problem which took his life in 1999. A great friend who we enjoyed so much was taken from our group. Yuma fun times were never quite the same with Pee Wee no longer with us.

***

We also were now starting to feel the effects of growing older. Maintaining the farm was always a joy for me and I kept the property looking like a park, but now some of that maintenance was getting to be a chore! In addition, a few tractor mishaps made me realize I was no longer as steady on my feet, and aching bones were a daily experience. We realized that in the near future, we would be unable to maintain our 110 acres and would probably have to sell the property. We also planned to have the entire family home in 1997 when we would celebrate our 50th wedding anniversary. Our anniversary would be on February 8 while we were in Yuma but we planned on a June celebration when all the family could be there.

When we returned home from delivering our Shadow Cruiser camper to British Columbia we began plans to put our property on the market in the spring. We returned to Yuma in the fall of 1996 and enjoyed the party times, games and visits with many of our friends.

We asked our friends Ron and Charlene Anderson to join us for dinner as we noted our wedding anniversary on February 8. On the way home, I surprised Jane with the following poem that our son, Paul, had framed for me and smuggled in our gear. The poem brought tears to Jane and Charlene. I guess I'm just a sentimental old guy!

TO JANE - ON OUR 50TH WEDDING ANNIVERSARY

The day that I first saw you
In nineteen forty-two
On the steps of Corpus Christi
I fell in love with you!

Now my steps are somewhat shaky
And some memories fade away
But my memory and thoughts of you
Are with me every day.

In February, at a dance
In nineteen forty-three
We met and danced, I took you home
'Twas a great day for me!

As I walked you home that cold, cold night
I was warm inside
For I knew that I had met the girl
Who would one day be my bride.

Those first few dates were special
With such a coy young Miss
For seven special dates, we had
Before I could steal a kiss!

In the war we separated

RAY RUBY

As I sailed upon the sea
Each day I thought of YOU and home
And how our life would be!

Then in nineteen forty-seven
On another cold, cold day
We made our pledge before our God
To LOVE, HONOR and OBEY!

As we stepped into our future
To begin our married life
That pledge would not be broken
As we were MAN and WIFE!

You gave to me, life's greatest gifts
Eight babies, born with pain
And through these many years of life
I've not heard you complain.

Now fifty happy years have passed
Since you became my wife
And I thank God I have you
Each day throughout my life!

I repeat the words that I first wrote you
Words that then, and now, are true
"IN THIS LITTLE POEM SWEETHEART
I'VE TOLD YOU OF MY LOVE FOR YOU!"

Happy Anniversary,
Jane,
I LOVE YOU!

***

We listed our farm for sale in late spring and made plans for our 50th wedding anniversary homecoming celebration for June when all the children could be there.

We also started checking out real estate on Tablerock Lake near Shell Knob, Missouri. Jane's cousin Herman Hanebrink and his wife Ardell, lived on the lake just out of Shell Knob and we really liked the area. After looking at many listings and rejecting some, we found a nice home on the Kings River arm of Tablerock, larger than we needed but a very well built home. We bought it.

Our farm sold quickly (probably priced too low). We enjoyed our 50th celebration with all the children, their families, many relatives and friends and immediately thereafter began the difficult task to prepare for a farm auction and the move to Tablerock.

We closed on the purchase of our home on Tablerock Lake on June 23, 1997, and closed on the sale of the farm on July 24, 1997. We moved the next day.

***

The years on Tablerock Lake were enjoyable and we made many good friends. We bought the pontoon boat from the sellers of our Kings River home, along with the covered boat slip on the lake. The pontoon was a very comfortable party rig but not well suited for the type of fishing which I enjoyed. We traded the pontoon for a Champion bass boat with an 80 horsepower motor. It proved too fast for this old guy and was difficult to steer unless the boat was fast on a plane. We had owned a number of boats in the past, and one of our favorites was an 18-foot Alumacraft walk through windshield with a 60 horsepower motor. We sold that boat to Lance Schwanke some years before but now looked for a similar design for greater comfort.

We continued to winter in Yuma, spending November through March there, returning in time for the white bass run on Tablerock Lake. The white bass must have learned that we moved on the lake since the white bass incredible spawning runs decreased significantly the year we purchased our property. We caught some nice white bass, but never encountered the fabulous runs of which everyone spoke.

The necessary moving from our summer residence to winter in Yuma, which involved utilities, mail, etc., was beginning to become a chore. We also knew that Ron and Charlene Anderson, our good friends, were considering the sale of their winter home in Yuma. We decided to sell and advertised in the local paper. I didn't want to make a profit so offered the home for what we paid plus the improvements we made. Three people wanted to buy it! I should have priced it higher. I agreed to sell to the first couple and the deal was closed. It turned out that the sale did not cover all of our improvements and we lost a little over $2000. We had some great winters in Yuma and made many lasting friends.

***

Edwin and Mary Gilsdorf were among our friends who wintered in Yuma. We often played pinochle with Ed and Mary and Ed's sister and brother-in-law, Dick and Leona Goheen. We usually went to breakfast together, to a Greek restaurant in Yuma, after attending the 8 a.m. Mass on Sunday. Ed and Mary lived in Sequim, Washington, on the Olympic peninsula and invited me to go salmon fishing with him. Ed owned an older motor home which he customized to a four wheel drive vehicle. He used this to tow his inboard fishing boat to an Indian reservation out of LaPush, Washington, on the west coast of the Olympic peninsula. Ed said that Jane and Mary could visit and shop while we fished. Ed's brother, Felix, a member of a Catholic religious order, would join us for the fishing trip. We agreed to go and arrived in Sequim on July 29, 2000. In the wee hours we received a phone call from Joan, my brother Joe's wife, that Joe had passed away after a long illness. Joan told us not to try to come home for the funeral. We had visited Joe often during his illness and his death was not unexpected.

It left another empty spot in my heart, and I will always miss and remember Joe and all of our family. The years in Farmington, with Mary and Harry living near the end of our lane, and Joe and Joan on their farm about six miles from us, were the most enjoyable years of our retirement. Now Hortense (Sis), Mary, Tom and I were the only ones left of the George J. Ruby family! That changed when on December 15, 2000 Sis passed away. We were iced in and unable to make it to her funeral. Sis was a real sweetheart, whom we loved and will always miss!

Ed, Felix and I packed the motor home and boat, and prepared for several days of fishing. Ed drove the motor home pulling the boat and Felix and I took Ed's pickup truck which would be used to launch Ed's boat. The first day of fishing produced some nice salmon as we fished about five miles or so off shore. Ed's boat was equipped with a GPS so navigation was assured.

The second day brought some fog and rough seas. With the GPS, we navigated to a spot where Ed had often fished with success. We caught our limit and I caught the largest salmon. We started for shore as the wind and waves were increasing. Felix was in the wheel house with Ed, as I started to clean and prepare some of our catch. Suddenly there was a loud crunch as the engine died! We hit something! Ed shouted that we had hit one of the lobster floats, which could not be seen due to the rough water. A line to the float was wrapped around our propeller, and since the line was attached to a large lobster trap, we were anchored in the ocean. The wind and waves were pushing the boat causing the stern to be in danger of shipping water which could cause us to sink. I volunteered to go over the stern to cut the rope to release us from this danger. Ed and Felix objected but there seemed to be no choice! Felix tied a line to my foot and I hung over the stern to reach the rope. Fortunately, the rope parted after cutting nearly through and this was accomplished without my getting very wet. The small lines were still wrapped around the propeller and I was able to untangle them with the use of a long boat hook. The engine was re-started, the prop was damaged, causing quite a vibration to the boat, but we reached the harbor OK.

I insisted on contributing to the repair of the prop and after a lot of resistance, Ed accepted. Mary and Jane drove over from Sequim and joined us for dinner that evening (they brought the dinner - it was the best meal of the trip). Our visit was most enjoyable and we were grateful for their hospitality. Ed passed away the following year. He was a great friend and will always be remembered and missed.

Mary and Harry sold their home in Farmington and rented an apartment in South St. Louis to be close to their two children. Mary had been suffering from Parkinson's disease for a number of years and the situation was becoming much worse. We looked for a nursing home for Mary since Harry's eyesight was failing and he could no longer provide the care which Mary needed. We found a nursing home near their apartment and Mary was admitted. Her health was failing rapidly and she could no longer walk. On my last visit to Mary we found that the home had placed a mattress on the floor to protect Mary from falling out of bed. Harry told us that she could no longer speak. I knelt down beside her and leaned close to her head as I said, "Mary, I sure love you!" She didn't open her eyes but very clearly said, "I love you too!" A large lump appeared in my throat and I could so longer speak! How I loved all of our family and the pain of their deaths remain with me always! Mary died on November 7, 2000.

***

We found the distance from St. Louis to Tablerock Lake was too great for any of the children to visit often and was also becoming more difficult for us to visit them. We considered buying a small home in the St. Charles County area and keeping the home on the lake, but that would mean maintaining two homes again, which we wanted to avoid. Gery found a house in Jonesburg, Missouri which would be about ten miles from acreage he and Joyce bought and on which they would build their permanent home. It would also be close to Paul and Barb in Foristell and they also were looking for some acreage near Jonesburg. The house Gery found needed extensive remodeling, which I didn't have the energy or will to do. Gery, Joyce, Paul, Barb, Donn, Mary Kay, Lori and family, all volunteered to take care of the necessary remodeling and we bought the property on January 29, 2001. They did an admirable job. It turned out just great, and we are indebted to all of them. We continue to receive compliments on the job they did!

Our home on Tablerock was listed for sale and sold on May 3, 2001, after which we moved to Jonesburg. This would be our final move! We now would be close to our Missouri children and their families. Lori and Mary Kay would be about one hour away. Gery and Joyce completed their home on Tower Road, about ten miles from us, and Paul and Barb purchased acreage about five miles from us on which they are constructing their permanent home. Both properties are picture book-perfect with lakes, privacy and great views. We are happy for them. Lori rents a nice farm house near Leslie, Missouri and enjoys the extra space for garden, etc. Donn and Mary Kay have a beautiful home in Creve Coeur, a suburb of St. Louis, so we get to see them quite often, which we appreciate. We visit by telephone regularly with Rita, Jean, John and Alan since the distance is too great for frequent visits. We do spend some time each summer visiting with John and family in Minnesota, which is about 700 hundred miles distant. John constructed a "bunk house" on his property where Jane and I stay when visiting. It is a cute little bunk house without all the modern conveniences, which takes me back to my childhood days. We enjoy it!

On October 26, 2002, we learned of the sudden and unexpected death of Catherine (Gillespie), Jane's only sister. Catherine was 84 years old. Catherine's husband 'Bud' predeceased her.

***

Jonesburg has a Catholic Church, St. Patrick's, which is served by visiting priests to provide one Mass on Sunday at 9 a.m. The congregation consists of many fine families who are dedicated workers and loyal to the parish. We missed having a resident priest and started to attend Mass on Tuesdays at Holy Rosary Church in Warrenton, which had Mother of Perpetual Help Devotions following the Mass. We liked the stability of the resident priest, the church and the members, so we now attend Holy Rosary regularly.

One Tuesday after Mass, we introduced ourselves to a cute girl named Julie Avis. When Julie heard our name, she said, "Ray

Ruby, we bought your big house on Hord Avenue in Jennings. My maiden name was Neske!" We of course remembered the Neske family, a great family of sixteen children. The first thing Julie asked if we ever saw any of the ghosts in the house on Hord. I described our experience while living there and related the incident with our son, Alan, which I mentioned in the early part of this book. Julie said that she would see three small girls who would sit on the floor and just look at her. She occupied the same bedroom where Alan saw the little boy. Julie would hide her eyes while repeating, "They are not real, mother said they aren't real," but when she would open her eyes they would still be there and finally vanish. I asked how these figures were dressed and she said they appeared in styles of clothing of long ago! Alan described the little boy as being strangely dressed! It seemed as though these spirits, or whatever they were, were fascinated by young children and wanted to be acquainted! We don't pretend to have any answers for these events but guess there are many things which we will never be able to explain or understand. We know this thirteen room three story house was occupied by a childless couple and his widowed sister for about 50 years prior to our purchase of the home. There were several owners prior to 1900. This house, now on the Historic Register, will always be a mystery to us!

***

If you read my first book, "Do Tell - Hear the Corn Grow," you will now have walked with me from the old hill farm in Chesterfield on Wild Horse Creek Road in 1929 through the 1930's, World War II and all the years to 2006. You have experienced my joys and my sorrows, and now probably know me quite well!

As I approach the final miles, I realize how blessed my life has been and thank God for the family into which I was born, the family of Jane and our eight wonderful children, their spouses, families and the many friends who have touched my life in the past 80 years. I will never forget you!

We have witnessed so many changes in the years since 1930, many positive and helpful, but we have lost much of what has made this country so great! We hope and pray that we can return to some of the moral standards of years now past - to respect life and all the gifts God has given us. We seem to have forgotten that with our "RIGHTS" we also have "OBLIGATIONS!" To express my strong thoughts on the subject of abortion, I wrote the following poem.

OUR RIGHTS

My county 'tis of THEE, we sing
A gift from God, our mighty king!
The "Bill of Rights," our guarantee
Of RIGHT TO LIFE and Liberty!

Our nation's SYMBOL soars on high,
The majestic Eagle, in the sky!
His RIGHT TO LIFE, our law defends
With justice swift, without amends!

Should one destroy an eagle's egg.
A plea for mercy, he must beg
From heavy fines and prison time -
Punishment for this tragic crime!

While across our land, from East to West
Human babies die within their nest
When mothers CHOOSE, this THING to do
Their "RIGHTS" and laws protect them, too!

Each day our SYMBOL soars on high
While thousands of human babies die!
If we cannot see this fallacy
Then God has drawn his grace from THEE!

***

RAY RUBY

The years remaining are a bonus and I am grateful for them and all the memories. I often picture our children as they were, small and all together. This poem describes the dream of an old man.

WHERE HAVE ALL MY BABIES GONE

In a cottage on a hillside
In an old oak rocking chair
Sat a very tired old man
With white and thinning hair.

His saddened eyes, now downcast
Were dimmed from many years -
He raised a weathered hand to cheek
To brush away some tears.

He wanted now to sleep a while
To rest his old, tired head -
But his lips began to move
And this is what he said:

"Where have all my babies gone?
Will I see them all once more?
Will I awake sometime from sleep
And see them standing at my door?

Will they all come forward
That I may hold them close to me
And see them all together -
Happy as they used to be.

Have I taught them anything
How to act, do and say?
Are they thankful for their blessings -
Do they ever kneel and pray?

Do they know how much I love them -
Will they walk both straight and tall
So if life should push them over
They quick recover from the fall!"

Then suddenly he heard and saw them -
His babies all around his chair -
Little hands and arms around him -
Laughing, smiling, everywhere!

In the morning, in his rocker,
They found his body, cold and still -
His lips not whispering their names now -
And they no longer will!

Where had all his babies gone?
They were never far away -
They were locked within his heart
And there forever, they will stay!

***

As I close the final chapter of this book, I wish to summarize the families of our eight children and acknowledge how proud I am of all of you as you pursue your respective careers and callings.

Rita Jane (Steve Ullrich): Julie; Brent;

Brent and Samantha (Whistler) - Daughter - Brea Danielle Jean Ann;

John - Sue (Hlavaty): John Raymond; Brian Wm.; Emily Michael;

John Raymond and Becky (Nice) - son John Ryan

Alan - Mary (Klein): Mark David; Kelly Elizabeth; Christopher Michael;

Paul - Barbara (Gentile): Anthony (Tony) Oliver; Stephanie Lynn; Jacob Thomas

Gery - Joyce (Capstick); Samantha Ann; Kristan Lee; Alicia Joy; and Emily Ruth Wallace (who later joined the family group.)

Mary Kay and Donn (Finkenkeller);

Lori (Darrin Ferguson); Amanda Kay; Coty Alan; Bobbie Ray;

May God continue to bless and keep you safe in his loving care.

THE END

Made in the USA